CONTENTS

Acknowledgements   ix

Notes on the Contributors   xi

Introduction   xiii

Chapter 1   **Microcomputers and the Curriculum — Uses and Abuses**   **1**
Vic Kelly

Some dangers of misuse   4
The educational potential of the microcomputer   8
'Good practice'   13
Summary and conclusions   19

Chapter 2   **Overcoming Computer-Induced Anxiety**   **20**
Leslie A. Smith

Self-doubt   21
    Information Technology and the curriculum   21
    Microcomputers and curriculum development   23
    Computers and anxiety   25
Self-help   31
    Keyboard experience   32
    The user guide   32
    Handling the equipment   33
    Pair-work and group-work   34
Summary and conclusions   35

Chapter 3   **Computers in the Primary Classroom**   **36**
David Dodds

Malpractice   36
'Good Primary practice'   38
Into practice — Why?   42
Into practice — How?   43
  Curriculum-centred uses   44
    Gibraltar Point Nature Reserve   44
    Abbeydale Industrial Hamlet   49
    Weather   53
  Curriculum innovation   55
  Curriculum support   59
Summary and conclusions   62

Chapter 4   **Learning Why to Hypothesize: a Case Study of Data Processing in a Primary School Classroom**   **64**
Alistair Ross

Hypothetico-deductive investigation   64
Social Studies   66
Hardware and software   68
  The survey   69
  Coding   71
  Analysis   73
Summary and conclusions   82

Chapter 5   **Why LOGO?**   **84**
Beryl Maxwell

Introducing the 'Floor Turtle'   86
Mathematics and the 'Turtle'   89
Further developments — beyond mathematics   96
Summary and conclusions   106

Chapter 6   **Micros and Mathematical Thinking**   **107**
Charles Bake

Sorting data   108
Mathematics lessons   111
Micros and thought processes   115

MICROCOMPUTERS AND THE CURRICULUM

MICROCOMPUTERS AND THE CURRICULUM

Edited by

A.V. Kelly

Harper & Row, Publishers
London

Cambridge San Francisco
Hagerstown Mexico City
Philadelphia São Paulo
New York Sydney

Copyright © 1984 Introduction, Chapter 1 and Chapter 9 A.V. Kelly: Chapter 2
Leslie A. Smith: Chapter 3 David Dodds: Chapter 4 Alistair Ross: Chapter 5
Beryl Maxwell: Chapter 6 Charles Bake: Chapter 7 Deryn Watson: Chapter 8
Evelyn Chakera.

First published 1984
All rights reserved

Harper & Row Publishers Ltd
28 Tavistock Street
London WC2E 7PN

British Library Cataloguing in Publication Data
    Microcomputers and the curriculum.
    1. Computer-assisted instruction — Great Britain
    2. Microcomputers — Great Britain
    I. Kelly, A.V.
    371.3'9445'0941   LB1028.5

    ISBN 0-06318-273-4

Typeset by Burns & Smith, Derby
Printed & bound by Butler & Tanner Ltd, Frome and London.

Developing mathematical thinking   115
Infants and micros   117
   Case study: BIGTRAK   117
   Case study: CRASH   121
   Case study: LOGO   121
Juniors and micros   122
   Case study: RHINO   122
   Case study: RAY BOX   123
   Case study: EUREKA   123
Summary and conclusions   124

Chapter 7   Microcomputers in Secondary Education — A Perspective with Particular Reference to the Humanities   125
Deryn Watson

The appearance of micros in schools   126
Classroom organization   127
The teacher's role   128
The determining factor — software   130
   The discipline base   130
   'What would happen if . . . ?'   131
   Model examination   132
   Hypothesis testing   133
   'What shall I do?'   134
   Games   134
Group dynamics   135
The interactive classroom   137
The database   137
Word processing   139
The curriculum response   140
   Evidence of current practice   140
   The Information Technology school   141
   A revolution   142
Summary and conclusions   144

Chapter 8   **Contrasting Approaches to the Learning
             Processes in Special Schools**   **145**
             Evelyn Chakera

             The contrasting roles of the learner and of the
                microcomputer within these two approaches   147
             Different learning styles   148
             Papert's approach to learning   149
             The investigation   152
             Discussion of the results of this investigation   157
             Summary and conclusions   161

Chapter 9   **In Conclusion**   **162**
             Vic Kelly

             Extending the teacher's powers   164
             The teacher's expertise   166
             A curriculum revolution?   169

Bibliography   **171**

List of Software   **177**

Acknowledgements   **180**

Author Index   **181**

Subject Index   **183**

ACKNOWLEDGEMENTS

As editor, I must acknowledge the help I received from all the contributors to this book. Promptness in responding to requests for copy or for amendments was not in every case a notable feature of our relationship, but throughout a happy state of collaboration existed without which the text could never have been completed in so short a time. Thanks are also due to my secretary, Jill Thorn, who has not only assisted in the production of typescript but has also done a good deal of efficient and productive stage-managing of the exercise on the many occasions when I have been involved elsewhere.

Vic Kelly

NOTES ON THE CONTRIBUTORS

Charles Bake is a teacher with special responsibility for mathematics, science and computing at Woodside Junior School in Croydon. He is regularly called upon to talk to teachers on INSET courses about the uses of microcomputers and software.

Evelyn Chakera is Acting Deputy Head of Fox Hollies School, Birmingham, a school for pupils, aged 4–19 years, with severe learning difficulties. Her interest in the use of microcomputers in the education of such pupils began when she undertook the investigation she describes in Chapter 8 as part of a Diploma course in the Further Education of Young People with Learning Difficulties. This interest was prompted by a conviction that more can and should be done for such pupils than to offer them mere training.

David Dodds is Headteacher of Thurcroft Junior School in Rotherham. His work there continues and extends the tradition of Primary education established in that part of the country by Sir Alec Clegg, and his interest in the use of microcomputers in education, as his chapter here clearly shows, springs from a conviction, which he has been able to demonstrate most effectively in practice, that they offer unprecedented opportunities to develop Primary education along the lines which that tradition has helped to set.

Vic Kelly is Dean of the School of Education at Goldsmiths' College. He also has special responsibility there for the advanced courses for experienced teachers and for the work in Curriculum Studies. He is rapidly becoming expert at getting other people to write books for him. This is not entirely due to laziness, or even to overwork, but is mainly a result of his conviction that the best, if not the only way towards the kind of educational development he wishes to see and to promote is through increased opportunities for the dissemination of ideas between teachers, particularly if these ideas can be supported by convincing accounts of the ways in which they have been translated into practice.

Beryl Maxwell has recently been appointed Head of the Hertfordshire Mathematics Centre. Previously, she worked for twelve years as a Primary Mathematics teacher at Crabtree Junior School, Harpenden. She was seconded for a term from here by the Advisory Unit for Computer Based Education, Hatfield, to work with Primary children and a Floor Turtle.

Alistair Ross is a classroom teacher at Fox Primary School, Notting Hill Gate, London. His responsibilities there are for the coordination of Social Studies throughout the school. He was recently seconded to work as advisory teacher for Social Studies and History in Primary schools in the Inner London Education Authority.

Leslie A. Smith is a Principal Lecturer in Education and Tutor-in-charge of In-service BEd courses at Goldsmiths' College. He has had extensive experience of working with teachers at both pre-service and in-service levels, and his main interest is in classroom-based curriculum innovation. He was formerly Head of the Curriculum Laboratory at Goldsmiths' College and, before that, Headmaster of a Secondary school in Essex.

Deryn Watson is Assistant Director (Humanities) of the Computers in the Curriculum Project, Chelsea College. After many years teaching Geography in London, she has become increasingly involved in the development of computer-assisted learning materials in history, geography, economics and languages. It is in the close relationship between CAL and the developing curriculum that her research interest lies through a wide range of contacts with teachers in the UK who form the Project's writing groups.

INTRODUCTION

This book is the product of a very rapid and brief survey of the use of microcomputers in schools which was undertaken as a result of three main convictions — first, that there is great educational potential in the microcomputer, secondly, that this potential is not often being tapped in the use currently being made of microcomputers in schools, and, thirdly, that a major reason for this failure is the absence of proper help for teachers in this area. All three of these hypotheses have been confirmed. The chapters which follow will reveal how and why.

The survey was prompted also by a consciousness of the need for something to be done very quickly in this area in response to the recent expansion of the use and availability of microcomputers in schools — and, indeed, in the homes of many pupils too.

The advent of the microcomputer and its ready accessibility to children both in their homes and at school are likely to lead to a major educational revolution. By 1984 every school in the country will have at least one machine. The Department of Industry, through the Department of Education and Science, is currently providing every institution concerned with the initial preparation of teachers with equipment to the value of £5000 and equipment to the value of a further £15,000 has been made available to selected institutions. Every attempt must, therefore, be made to ensure that teachers are able to familiarize themselves with computer technology and especially with its educational potential.

How this potential is envisaged will be crucial to the development of education and will determine the form any revolution will take — indeed, it will determine whether there will be a revolution at all, whether there will be a fundamental rethinking of educational values and principles of a kind the new technology invites or merely some modifications in educational methodology. For there are several ways in which the microcomputer can be used in schools. In some schools, teachers have established Computer Studies courses which consist largely of the learning of a computer language — usually BASIC — and of techniques of computer programming. It is also clear from developments which have already taken place that a major feature of its current use is as a sophisticated teaching aid, a device to enhance and perhaps accelerate learning of a traditional kind. Thus in many schools teachers have designed or purchased programs for the learning of certain aspects of their subjects and the pupils merely work through these. The microcomputer is thus seen as little more than a new and highly efficient form of teaching machine. In other schools it seems as though it is seen as offering little beyond an extension of the opportunities for video games most pupils already enjoy at home. Thus, as has so often unfortunately been the case with educational television, it is used as a device for keeping children quiet and occupied; possibly it develops some kinds of manipulative skill, but any educational merits that might go beyond this are not recognized. In an interesting way, these two approaches reflect two paradigms of educational philosophy or perhaps caricatures of the two extremes of education theory — the one concerned merely with the acquisition of knowledge, the second with largely unstructured and undirected activity and play.

A third possible use of the microcomputer, however, can be seen as relating to a third model of education — that of education as experience, as active learning, as a matter of processes rather than products. For the major advantage of the microcomputer is not that it can think for one but that it can make one think, so that its potential for promoting the development of children's thought processes is enormous.

> The teaching machines of computer-assisted instruction transferred declarative knowledge with assembly-line efficiency but did nothing to upset the stale notion that learning is little more than the acquisition of facts. Software programs of today, on the other hand, teach process: not new skills per se but how to learn new skills, even how to think. Indeed, modern Piagetians believe that computers allow children to conduct their research about the world on a scale never before possible in a sandbox or a playground. (Rheingold 1983, p.38)

This is the essence of the revolution which the microcomputer makes possible. It is described by Howard Rheingold in the same paper as 'in effect, bringing the seminal thinking of John Dewey and Jean Piaget into the age of the silicon chip' (ibid.). Such a revolution, however, only becomes possible if children are encouraged and enabled to make full use of the microcomputers rather than being 'programmed' by them. For it is 'a revolution in ideas that is no more reducible to technologies than . . . poetry to the printing press' (Papert 1980, p.186). If this potential remains untapped, if only because it goes unappreciated, a major force for educational advance will have been lost and the use or misuse made of computer technology in education may well even prove counter-productive to such advance.

The prime intention of this book, then, is to attempt to reveal to teachers and to others what this potential might be and how it might be attained. To achieve this we offer a series of contributions which interlink theoretical discussion and practical examples in such a way as to demonstrate both the kinds of thinking which we believe teachers should be engaging in when facing up to the demands and pressures of this new development and some of the ways in which that thinking has been translated into practice. In general, in this field as in most areas of education, problems arise, inadequacies occur, opportunities are lost, not only through bad practice but also, and more often, through bad theory, or rather through that bad practice which results from bad theory, from a failure to provide an adequate theoretical underpinning for practical decisions and action. The truth of this in relation to the use of microcomputers in schools will be apparent from what follows. What will also emerge, however, is the corollary of this — namely, that good practice can only occur if there is a basis of good theory, that proper thinking or theorizing about one's practice is as important as having the practical skills to implement one's plans, that, specifically in this context, thinking about the educational potential of the microcomputer is at least as important as possessing the skill to operate the equipment confidently and competently.

The first chapter, then, describes some of the dangers which may arise when teachers begin to use microcomputers with their pupils or to introduce them into their curricular provision without giving adequate thought to their educational value and potential. It goes on to identify some of the major features of that potential as a basis for an attempted definition of what might constitute 'good practice' in this field, what might be the essential criteria against which we should be evaluating work in this area.

One of the reasons why this potential so often goes unrecognized and thus untapped is, of course, the inevitable lack of expertise of most teachers in this area. It is quite clear, even from this brief survey, that this is an area in which at present greater and more extensive expertise is to be found among the pupils than among the teachers. One might, therefore, want to question the wisdom of spending large sums of public money on providing the hardware without first ensuring that an adequate number of teachers had been enabled to acquire the necessary expertise to make proper use of it. Some effort has been made in this direction, especially by those concerned with the Microcomputers in Education Project, but in spite of this the lack of teacher expertise is a major factor which must be reckoned with in a survey of this kind. It is to this problem, then, that Leslie Smith devotes himself in Chapter 2, where he first of all attempts to reassure those many teachers who may suffer the anxiety that such lack of expertise and understanding brings, if only by revealing that there are good reasons for those feelings and that they are shared by many of their colleagues, and he then goes on to suggest ways in which they might begin to develop the kind of expertise which will dispel their anxiety. Future generations of teachers will not face this problem; for they will have grown up in the computer age and should have acquired some expertise during their courses of teacher education. It is the teachers in the schools now who need help. This chapter, and, indeed, this book is an attempt to offer it.

We then move on to look at the work of some teachers who do have this expertise and have also the kind of understanding of the educational process which has enabled them to use it to forward a range of educational goals. It is perhaps inevitable that such teachers are more often to be found in the Primary sector of our education system than elsewhere; for it is there that teachers have long enjoyed greater scope for developing their ideas; it is consequently there that the most interesting curriculum development has occurred and it is there that a more imaginative approach to education has been invited and encouraged officially by two major reports, those of the Hadow (1931) and the Plowden (1967) committees.

Thus we have four contributions from teachers in this sector and they add up to a comprehensive outline of the potential of the microcomputer in the Primary school. For David Dodds describes many of the ways in which he has been able to use the microcomputer to extend the range and the scope of the, already very interesting, work he has been doing with his delightful young pupils at Thurcroft Junior School near Rotherham. His contribution, Chapter 3, demonstrates very clearly what the potential of the microcomputer is when teachers come to see it, and to use it, as an educational tool rather than as a gimmick, as a very powerful slave rather than an inhuman master. Alistair Ross then takes up the story in Chapter 4 and shows that what is needed is for teachers to give a good deal of thought to, in order to be quite clear about, the kinds of process education requires them to support and promote. For this will then provide them with a theoretical basis upon which to build their curricular provision generally, and specifically it will enable them to see, as he shows most compellingly through an account of some of his own work, what suitable roles the microcomputer can play in this enterprise. In Chapter 5, Beryl Maxwell asks the question 'Why LOGO?' and sets out to describe how she was won over to the use of the microcomputer with her pupils by an encounter with LOGO and how she has subsequently developed her work and that of her pupils in the area of mathematical thinking in some very interesting ways. Finally, in Chapter 6, Charles Bake takes us on to an exploration of the contribution of the microcomputer in this same particular area of the curriculum, the development of mathematical thinking. In doing so, he also reveals the possibilities that exist for interesting work with children at the Infant level, for whom the concrete experiences of working with BIGTRAK combined with the more abstract forms of CRASH and LOGO's 'screen turtle' can provide a base for the development of many of those spatial concepts which are so necessary to the growth of mathematical thinking.

Perhaps one of the most interesting points which emerges from all four of these contributions is that most of the work they describe is not such as to demand high levels of computer expertise from teachers (although it does require a high level of educational expertise). This must be reassuring to those teachers who suffer from that computer-induced anxiety that Leslie Smith discusses in Chapter 2. For, just as pupils do not need to learn an elaborate computer language to 'talk' productively to the microcomputer, so teachers do not need it to use the microcomputer effectively in an educational context. Primary teachers, then, and perhaps all teachers, must find these chapters reassuring as well as exciting in the potential they describe for work with younger pupils.

It proved more difficult to find examples of similarly interesting work in Secondary schools. In many of these, the use of the microcomputer is confined to the Mathematics Department. Many of them too have established Computer Studies courses. These are, of course, valuable developments, but they are not such as to illustrate our theme of the educational use of the microcomputer and there were few examples to be found of this kind of use in Secondary schools. It seemed to make good sense, therefore, to settle for some broad perspectives on what is going on in this sector, especially in the Humanities, and this is what Deryn Watson provides in Chapter 7 from the perspective of her work with the Computers in the Curriculum project. A number of different kinds of development are outlined there, representing important and striking forms of rethinking, along with illustrative descriptions of some of the programs which have been produced to support these developments. There is a good deal here to promote productive discussion and debate among all teachers, but especially those who are interested in the potential offered by microcomputers in the field of Secondary education.

The possible uses of the microcomputer in Special Education must also be explored. For there would seem to be at least a *prima facie* case for suggesting that its potential for assisting pupils with learning difficulties may be enormous. Certainly, one can see its possibilities in facilitating learning in cases where pupils are hampered by some physical defects and even by intellectual deficiencies. However, the dangers of assigning to the microcomputer a mere teaching-machine or 'drill and practice' role in this sector of education are clearly greater than they are elsewhere and must be resisted as energetically if we are not to settle for that 'basic skills' approach to teaching and that emphasis on behaviour modification which have characterized so much of the theory and practice of education at this level. It is for this reason that one looks with interest at the experiment described by Evelyn Chakera in Chapter 8, an experiment in which she attempted to promote the intellectual development of some severely retarded adolescents by using BIGTRAK and the LOGO 'Floor Turtle'. The main interest of this experiment is that it attempted to develop the education of those pupils not from that standpoint of behaviourist psychology which has too long dominated educational planning in this field, but from a cognitive/developmental perspective which emphasizes a concern with their conceptual development. It is a small experiment, but it points the way towards something which might be very important in the emancipation of pupils of this kind from the limitations of behaviour modification. A major conclusion of this chapter would seem to be not just that the potential of the microcomputer in this sector of education is as great as one might suppose, but again that, if we are to tap that potential, there must be a major rethinking about educational provision in that sector and the basic principles of that provision.

This reflects what was said earlier in this Introduction about the need for a major overhaul of our thinking about education generally in the light of the development of computer technology. This is in many ways the central message of this book. For, although it is our prime concern to help teachers to think how they might take full educational advantage of the opportunities offered by the microcomputer and how they might translate that thinking into action, our underlying theme is that this will necessitate a rethinking of many of our educational principles. The advent of the microcomputer is something no-one can afford to ignore; it is something no teacher can afford to ignore. It is a major development for society and it is a major development for education. It will change our jobs in its own way if we do not take control and use it to change them in ours.

CHAPTER 1

MICROCOMPUTERS AND THE CURRICULUM — USES AND ABUSES

VIC KELLY

It is now 40 years since Harold Benjamin in his amusing and illuminating paper, 'The Saber-Tooth Curriculum' (1939), suggested that the curriculum had so far lagged behind the general development of our western culture as to have reached the point of making a positive virtue out of initiating the young into the major elements of a culture long outgrown and outdated. In the mythical society depicted in that paper the 'educational' activities or subjects into which the young were introduced were those skills which had been essential to the economy of their ancestors — 'fish-grabbing-with-the-bare-hands', 'woolly-horse-clubbing' and 'saber-tooth-tiger-scaring-with-fire'. These skills now having lost the utilitarian value of the past had become the main ingredients of the 'liberal education' of the present. It is not difficult to see the parallel with major elements of the curriculum of many schools, especially at Secondary level, at the time at which that paper was written.

Since that time, however, we have passed through several phases of the 'curriculum development' era. The message of that paper, that we must think about our curricular offerings and find better justification for them than mere hallowed antiquity, has been taken to heart and there has been a plethora of discussions of curricular issues, at all levels, both professional and lay, and (whether consequently or merely contemporaneously it would be rash to say), a certain amount of change also in the actual curricula of many schools. Some of this change has been designed to render what is offered more relevant to contemporary society — this was the major message of Benjamin's paper. Some of it has, therefore, lost sight of an aspect of education which that paper largely ignored, namely that usefulness or utility is not the only criterion of educational value — indeed, it may genuinely not be a criterion at all. Some of it, therefore, has represented a swing of the pendulum in the opposite direction; a move from the non-utilitarian to the utilitarian, and even from the values of the past to the values of the future — from the 'saber-tooth' curriculum to the '2001' curriculum — a swing which may well bring with it its own unsatisfactory consequences for curriculum planning.

Nowhere is this shift more apparent than in the uses being made by schools of the new microchip technology. For it is clear that in many places teachers and schools are embracing it as avidly for its 'futuristic' attractions as once they embraced the study of the ancient world for the traditional values enshrined there. In both cases, there is a failure to evaluate the curriculum in terms of its educational merits and value here and now.

It is the purpose of this chapter to argue that the use of microcomputers in schools does not in itself guarantee the existence of a satisfactory educational curriculum, any more than the inclusion of Latin or Greek or Ancient History does or did. It is always necessary to ask some searching questions about *how* things are taught or used and to evaluate this against some agreed educational criteria. It is the intention, therefore, to try to identify some of the ways in which current approaches to the use of microcomputers in schools are going wrong, largely because of the failure to ask these questions, to draw attention to some of the many educational advantages that offer themselves when the potential of the microcomputer is evaluated in these terms and, in the light of these, to offer a definition of what might be seen as 'good practice' in this area. Subsequent chapters will elaborate on this last point in considerable detail.

A preliminary point needs to be made, however, before we attempt to review existing uses of the microcomputer in schools and that concerns the importance of ensuring that schools do come to terms, in one way or another, with this major form of technological development, that they do begin to concern themselves with the development of computer literacy. Computer technology is now a major part of everyone's everyday life. It is a computer which tells us whether we may or may not have money on our banker's checkpoint or credit card; it is a computer which totals up our gas, electricity or telephone bill and our expenditure in most shops, supermarkets and petrol stations; it is a computer which calculates the amount of benefit we are entitled to if we are unemployed; it is a computer which produces for us much of the data we need, or at least like to have, in our work and play — from cricket scores, averages, run-rates etc. to chemical analyses. Much of everyone's leisure time is now spent in activities which are in some sense, if not directly, computer-based; few people's jobs are unaffected by microtechnology; and, indeed, we need not look far beyond the microcomputer to discover why some people no longer have jobs, as the recent advertisement for Fiat cars 'built entirely by robots', makes clear.

It is probably no exaggeration to suggest that this represents the most dramatic source of change since the Industrial Revolution. And it must be remembered that technological change of any kind leads inevitably to matching forms of social change, change not only in the material conditions of our lives but also in the values and social structures which those material conditions give birth to. Dramatic technological change, therefore, means equally dramatic social change, as the history of recent times makes very clear, and it is for this reason that education must be centrally involved in the process. The first Industrial Revolution was a major factor in the establishment of state education for all and in the corresponding introduction of a utilitarian element into thinking about education. The impact of current technological development, the third Industrial Revolution, is likely to be equally far-reaching in its effects on education and it is not too fanciful to speculate that the new thrust may well be in the opposite direction — away from the emphasis on acquiring the skills to perform tasks which the microcomputer can do much more easily and readily than we can ourselves and towards a concern for the development of those conceptual 'skills' which people are better at, and for the enrichment of life which now becomes possible.

It would exemplify a completely 'saber-tooth' attitude of mind, then, if, in planning a curriculum, we were to ignore this major dimension of the society we live in and of our pupils' everyday existence. Our schools would become even more unreal and irrelevant to our pupils if they were the only computer-free environment they found themselves in. It is right and proper, therefore, that microcomputers should be as widely available in schools as possible. The only criticism that can be made of the present arrangements to create this availability for all pupils is that money has been spent on the equipment and its accompanying software before it has been possible to prepare teachers for their proper use and to help them to think through their implications. It is this that has led to the misuses to which we must now turn, and it must be stressed at once that these are a matter of concern not merely because they represent missed opportunities but also because they offer some very positive dangers.

Some dangers of misuse

The dangers inherent in some of the approaches to the use of microcomputers in schools, those approaches I am about to define as misuses, are not hard to identify nor are they hard to find in current practice.

The first and most general point to be noted here is the absence of any curricular dimension from both the theory and the practice. Most of the papers which have been rushed into print in an attempt to meet the teachers' need for assistance in this area have lacked a deep theoretical perspective. They have concentrated their attention on what teachers might or should be doing with microcomputers and how they can do these things, but have too often failed to face up to the question of *why* they should do these things in these ways. They have tended to adopt a simplistic and naive model of education and of curriculum planning. In this, of course, they reflect much of what continues to go on in schools, especially in Secondary schools, where practice without theory is often the norm. But this means that they are leading us straight into the kinds of deficiency which that approach leads to, activities which lack obvious purpose and meaning except within the very narrow context in which they are conceived. While this may be understandable in areas which have the backing of tradition, it is somewhat bizarre as a basis for introducing something new and supposedly forward-looking. In short, it is the '2001' syndrome we have already noted. Thus the message of much of the literature is that we should use this technology because it is there and is available, that we should learn how to use it, that we should teach children how to use it, that — in the context of the Infant school — no child is too young to be taught how to use it, that — in the context of Special Education — no child is too handicapped to be taught how to use it. But little attention is given to the related questions of what we are all to use this technology for, how it is to be used to further our educational purposes or how it relates to the other kinds of activity or experience we continue to offer. These are questions which clearly are of concern to some teachers but they have not always been the focal points of attention for the 'experts'. In short, there is a major lack of a curriculum dimension to the debate.

This is reflected in, and/or reflects, the practice of many schools. It is not unusual to find schools offering computer studies as a subject on no more clearly thought out grounds than that 'society needs computer experts'. One is reminded of what used to be (and no doubt in some places still is) the recurring argument for the teaching of theoretical physics in schools to pupils of all kinds. Or one hears that 'in today's society children need to learn how to handle and use the microcomputer'. This is a slightly more compelling argument but would be more convincing if associated with a similar claim for the need to consider the role of the microcomputer in society rather more critically than is the case when one is merely being taught the language and/or the mechanics of it. It is also, of course, an argument which could be used with equal, or even greater, force of the need to provide driving lessons.

Then there are schools where the microcomputer is used in the way that 'educational' TV has often been used, as little more than a device for keeping some children quietly absorbed for long periods of time, where the motivational advantages of the small screen are used as a device for discipline and control rather than to any educational advantage. Thus children are permitted, encouraged even, to play computer games or to work through computer programs which are every bit as trivial, although perhaps not as obviously so, as those they play in the arcades, in the chip shops, in many other such places they may find themselves in, and often now in their own homes.

Finally, there are the schools which see the advantages of microcomputers in terms of nothing more than their being highly sophisticated teaching machines. There is nothing wrong with this approach in itself. Indeed, if a pupil can acquire some necessary knowledge and understanding more efficiently in this way than by any other it would be foolish to reject it. There are several dangers inherent in this kind of approach, however, which are not always clearly borne in mind.

Firstly, it is a very limited and limiting use of the microcomputer so that, if this is all we do with them, as was suggested in the Introduction (p.xiv) we are missing out on most of what they have to offer. Secondly, this kind of approach reinforces what I can only call the '39 steps' model of teaching. For it assumes that the kind of learning we should be concerned with in schools is solely, or at least largely, the acquisition of the kind of knowledge that can be offered in a linear, stage-by-stage, form. Thus it tends to rely too heavily on long-outmoded behaviourist theories of learning and to ignore some of the more interesting aspects of learning to which other schools of psychology have drawn our attention.

One of those more interesting aspects of learning is its social dimension, which many psychologists have recently encouraged us to stress in our teaching as being not only important in its own right but as a basis for effective learning. A third problem, however, with the teaching-machine approach to the use of microcomputers in the school is that it can, and perhaps must, encourage rather solitary, impersonal, even antisocial forms of learning. Children can, as we shall see later, join together in using a microcomputer, but it is difficult to see how far this can be done when a straight 'teaching-machine' use is envisaged. Thus the solitary, antisocial aspect of the home computer, which often receives more of a person's attention than parents, spouse, children or even guests these days, and the video game in the 'pub' bar, which often takes people away, sometimes for long periods, from the friends they are there to meet, begins to invade the school. The use by many programs of a smiling face on the screen as a reward for a correct answer to a question is an implicit acknowledgement of the importance of human interaction in learning, and thus represents an inherent contradiction in this kind of use of the microcomputer.

The question must also be asked, if we take this to its logical conclusion, why do children need to attend school for this kind of learning. Why should they not receive it at home through Prestel or Ceefax? And how far are we away from E.M. Forster's vision in *The Machine Stops* of a society in which we all live in our own private cells and communicate only by means of advanced technology? It is an approach that begins to look more like computers using or programming children than children using or programming computers. And it encourages one to question the value of using a microcomputer, whose capacity for storing information is almost limitless, to help children to store information when their capacity in this respect is clearly inferior. Given the information storage and retrieval capability of the microcomputer, the only reason why human beings should be required to store information is as a basis for the development of understanding. This is a principle which too often is lost.

Thus the problems of 'misuse' of the microcomputers are not confined to loss of the opportunities a proper use offers. There are dangers in the forms of misuse. The very advantages that the microcomputer offers will, at least for a time, ensure that these disadvantages do not become apparent. For the fascination of the machines, the absorption and the high level of motivation which offer such potential to the teacher will also ensure that schools will get away with their misusage; that it will be some time before children react against it. For, to repeat a recent comment from Frank Smith, perhaps the greatest potential danger of the microcomputer is that it can make the trivial seem, or even become, totally interesting and thus to appear to be of great importance. The transcription of some programs currently on offer from the screen to the ordinary, humble work-card will quickly demonstrate the truth of this — especially if they are then offered to pupils in this far less exciting form. We must remember that, if this is how we use the microcomputer, then most of the software available to us consists of what we might call 'electronic worksheets'. Viewed in that light, many of them will be seen to be not very sophisticated worksheets.

This draws our attention to a further, more important, and perhaps more sinister, aspect of this approach to the use of microcomputers in schools. Not only does much of the software currently available offer pupils trivia, it also, inevitably, exposes them to a particular set of values, a particular ideology. For built into the content of any program through the selection of that content and the manner of its presentation, will be the values, the ideology of the programmer, so that while we may feel that the microcomputer is helping Jill and Johnny to learn history more quickly and efficiently, we must recognize that it is helping them to learn a good deal more besides. This, of course, is true of every textbook, work-card, film, television programme or other externally prepared presentation we offer to our pupils, and we need to be aware that there are similar caveats to be raised there. What makes the matter especially serious in the case of programs prepared for use on microcomputers is that these are seldom as directly mediated by the teacher as most other forms of presentation can be. This is in part due to the nature of these programs, in part to the present level of competence in this area of most teachers, and is not entirely unrelated to the point we have just noted concerning the solitary nature of much learning of this kind.

No material of this kind can, of course, be neutered, nor would one want it to be. Indeed, it is not difficult to recognize that the whole process of education, however it is envisaged, must include exposure to different values and must involve a change in one's own attitudes and values. It is for this reason that educational theorists from Plato on have stressed the moral dimension of education and recognized that moral development constitutes a major part of becoming educated. What is wrong with the kind of exposure to the implicit ideologies of the software that has just been described is that it is usually largely uncritical, that it is a mostly unrecognized by-product of the learning which is planned, that it often takes the form of a largely unconscious influencing of one's attitudes and values and that it thus transgresses what many would argue to be another essential principle of the educational process, its concern with the development of powers of conscious critical awareness. Pupils must be encouraged, then, to question critically the implicit ideology and values of what we present to them. This seldom happens where the microcomputer is being used as a teaching machine.

Some important questions need to be asked, therefore, about much current practice in schools. In general, these are the same questions one ought to be asking about all educational practice and, fundamentally, they are curricular questions, those that encourage us to accept nothing just because it is there, to take as read the value of nothing, but to evaluate everything against a clear analysis of what we mean by the curriculum and, indeed, what we see as being essential to education.

We may be in a better position to do this when we have considered some of the potential advantages of the microcomputer in schools as these emerge both from thinking about the machines themselves and from considering the practice of those schools which have used them more productively.

The educational potential of the microcomputer

Perhaps the most serious of the criticisms I have just offered of some kinds of current use of microcomputers in schools is that these uses reflect a narrow view of the possibilities of this development and thus fail to tap its full educational potential. Even to an untutored eye that potential is tremendous. For the power that microtechnology has given to commerce and industry can be available to the teacher too and this is why the question of the proper use of such power becomes all-important and why, too, examples of its misuse become all the more disturbing.

It must be stressed at the outset that in all of what follows a particular view of what is educationally worth while is assumed and the educational potential of the microchip is outlined in terms of that particular view. If justification for this is needed, it is to be found firstly in the fact that nothing could ever be written about education which did not make some kinds of assumption about what it is or ought to be and which did not therefore base itself on some set of educational values. The notion of a scientific study of or statement about education is a complete myth; it is also highly dangerous since it encourages the adoption of approaches whose hidden assumptions remain unquestioned. Secondly, the assumptions made here are not such as to be regarded by most people as in any sense highly idiosyncratic. They are assumptions which, in my view, underlie the thinking (although perhaps not always the practice) of most teachers and, indeed, of many other people who have views on education.

For, fundamentally the assumption is made that education in the full sense goes some way beyond the mere acquisition of knowledge or of certain skills, that essentially it is a process which is concerned with some kind of personal development which is the result of the acquisition of this knowledge and those skills, and that this development is of a moral, social and emotional kind and is not restricted to the intellectual. Such a process will therefore involve the growth of understanding as well as the acquisition of knowledge, it will include the development of a system of values as well as of a cognitive perspective, and it will entail, as a corollary of all this, the ability to make a continuing critical review of one's knowledge, one's understanding and one's moral and social values. Such a process is best forwarded, therefore, not by teaching of a straight didactic kind, which can so readily and so often lead to the acquisition of knowledge of a kind which in no sense becomes fully a part of one's being or has any impact on one's view of life, which remains at the level of those 'inert ideas' which A.N. Whitehead (1932) warned us of; it can only be promoted by forms of learning in which the mind of the learner is actively engaged, in which there is genuine interaction and interplay between the learner and the activities he is engaged in, in which those activities, in short, become genuine experiences to which a genuinely personal response is invited and encouraged. This in turn suggests that any material we present to pupils must be relevant to them, encouraging them to see it as interesting for its own sake, must offer a challenge to their understanding, by confronting them with a problem to solve and thus creating what the developmental psychologists call 'cognitive dissonance', and must encourage them to ask their own questions rather than merely respond to ours. For there is little educational merit, and indeed little merit of any kind, in encouraging pupils to learn answers before they have 'learnt' the questions — to learn answers to questions whose significance they cannot see and which indeed may have no significance for them. It is with the asking of questions rather than the learning of answers that true education begins. It is to this kind of process that, in the view of the author, microtechnology has a major contribution to make. There are a number of reasons for making this claim.

Reference has already been made to the first of these, the power of the microcomputer to motivate and to absorb one's attention. The level of concentrated involvement that one sees from most children when engaged with a microcomputer, or, indeed, which one experiences oneself when similarly engaged, is something that no teacher can fail to be impressed by. A degree of motivation which would be regarded as exceptional in any other context becomes commonplace in this. Given the proper concern of all teachers in achieving a high level of motivation in their pupils, this advantage is not to be dismissed lightly.

On the other hand, we must recognize that the motivation apparently inherent in the microcomputer may not be the most appropriate kind of motivation and there may be dangers in accepting it at face value. For it is equally important to achieve an appropriate kind of motivation, and the kind of motivation which seems most appropriate to the sort of process we have just suggested education is will be one that is based on the intrinsic interest of the experience rather than on some extrinsic reward or advantage it might seem to offer. Again, it does appear that this high level of involvement of pupils engaged with microcomputers is a result of features inherent in the activity, the immediate rewards and satisfaction to be gained from the activity itself rather than from what it may lead to. This would seem to be, therefore, a further attraction to anyone concerned with the kind of educational process we have described.

A major reason for this level of involvement is, of course, that, unlike the television screen, the VDU will not permit the pupil to be a passive recipient (or possibly non-recipient) of what it is offering. If there is no response, it will not proceed. In fact, if there is no appropriate response, it will not proceed. Herein, then, is to be found a second major attraction for the educator. For here lies the possibility of fostering that active form of learning we are advocating. There must be interplay or interaction between pupil and the program; the pupil is required to think and to respond. Again, however, it is the nature and quality of the response required which is crucial. To be required to respond merely by offering the answer the program expects and demands involves a minimal level of active involvement, hardly more effective than responding to the kinds of closed question that many teachers pose in oral lessons. The full development of the pupil's cognitive powers demands a more sophisticated form of active engagement with the material than this and it was for this reason that we offered our earlier criticism of the use of the microcomputer as a teaching-machine. The point that is being stressed here is that the microcomputer offers us the possibility of a far more satisfactory form of active involvement. And this is a further major aspect of its educational potential. It can encourage and demand the right kind of constructive questioning and active interchange with educative material from every individual pupil.

This brings us to a third educational advantage of the microcomputer — it can interact with the pupil not merely by posing quesions and offering information, but also by handling and processing both the questions and the information the pupil on his or her part puts to it. The potential exists for a genuine interchange. Furthermore, the advantage the microcomputer has over the teacher here is not confined to the possibility of its being more readily available for a one-to-one or small-group interchange; it also has the capability for processing far more complex data and at a vastly superior speed. In other words, properly handled, the microcomputer can respond to pupils' questions with a degree of sophistication no teacher could ever hope to match and thus give access to kinds and levels of understanding which would otherwise remain inaccessible. Thus some of the most productive uses of microcomputers in schools to be found at present, as several of the chapters which follow will show, are those where this data-processing capability has been used to the utmost advantage and pupils — individually, in small groups or as whole classes — have been encouraged to collect their own data, prepare it for consumption by the microcomputer, feed it in and then pose a range of questions, all of their own devising, which the machine can respond to through an analysis of the data the pupils themselves have provided it with and the communication of such data in an altered form. Thus, at all stages, there is active involvement, in an activity whose relevance is constantly apparent, and to a productive end, namely the processing of data one has collected oneself in order to answer, or at least shed light on, questions one is posing oneself. The processing of information in order to enhance understanding is a major part of becoming educated. The microcomputer is a highly sophisticated device for doing just that — provided that we use it properly.

The ability to frame hypotheses for problem-solving and to test them in a suitable way is also an important element in educational development, and what we have just described can be seen also as offering a means for the immediate testing of such hypotheses. Subsequent chapters will show how the microcomputer can be used to explore even three-dimensional problems and their possible solutions. This is a further example of the active learning opportunities the microcomputer can provide.

There are at least two further aspects of this that need to be stressed. The first of these is that, apart from handling data in a far more sophisticated manner and at a far more rapid rate than either teacher or pupil could hope to achieve, the microcomputer can also take over and thus remove some of those complicated calculations which, as every teacher knows, so often stand in the way of the development of the kind of conceptual understanding which is the fundamental concern. For example, by taking the complicated mathematical calculations out of a topic such as food and dietary planning in Home Economics, the microcomputer can offer direct access to the real content of the subject and to the processes, the concepts, the understanding the teacher is primarily concerned to promote. In short, it can be left to do some of the chores, giving more time for both teacher and pupil to concentrate on what is really important. It can bypass the mathematical weakness of some pupils and provide direct access to the real content, process, concepts of a subject.

Secondly, it can help to reduce these important concepts to manageable proportions. It can offer what Seymour Papert (1980, Chapter 6) calls 'powerful ideas in mind-sized bites'. For while the microcomputer can handle data in far larger quantities than the human mind, it can digest it in helpings of a size the human mind can cope with and can offer it back, in response to our questions, in equally digestible portions. Nowhere is this so apparent as in those examples (some of which are described in the chapters which follow) in which, for instance, extensive census details have been gathered together by pupils and fed into a microcomputer to provide a database for subsequent analysis. On the basis of this analysis specific questions have been posed and answered and not only new knowledge acquired but also new levels of understanding achieved of a size and kind tailored to the pupils' capabilities. It would be difficult to imagine a more effective means of assisting pupils towards the development of a sense of history, a sense of social living, especially through insight on a different age, and even an understanding of social development.

Again, this may be seen as one aspect of the power the microcomputer has to extend pupils' horizons in so many ways. It is this potential that has been recognized by some teachers in Special Education as having a particular relevance for the problems handicapped pupils face in attaining the kinds of educational development more readily available to others. Properly used, the microcomputer can extend the handicapped pupils' range of possible experiences and enhance the educational opportunities which can be provided for him or her.

It will also be seen from what follows that the microcomputer offers opportunities for assisting the development of children's thinking from the concrete to the abstract, from the iconic to the symbolic. The notion of stages of intellectual development has been perhaps the most important contribution made by psychology to education and the claim that the child's thinking is *qualitatively* different from that of the educated adult is a crucial one for proper educational practice. For it requires of us both that we recognize the qualitative difference of the child's intellectual response to experiences and, more importantly, that we plan our work in such a way as not only to reflect such a recognition but also to promote the development of the child's thinking towards that of the mature and educated adult. One, perhaps rather simple, example of this is that it suggests that we recognize the dependence of young children on the concrete and assist them to develop the ability to handle abstract modes of thinking and to achieve the highest possible levels of conceptual understanding. In subsequent chapters, we will see teachers promoting this process most effectively through the use of microcomputers. The most obvious example of this is in the use of LOGO, where young children, and handicapped children too, can be seen to move, sometimes quite rapidly and usually quite spontaneously, from the concrete experience provided by using a 'Floor Turtle' to the rather more abstract intellectual/conceptual levels of understanding demanded by the 'Screen Turtle'. There are, however, other more complex examples of this and other related processes also to be found in what follows. If one accepts a view of education which sees this kind of development as crucial, then, one cannot but be impressed by the potential the microcomputer offers here.

A final point that must be made is that the processes or procedures we are describing here require, almost as a spin-off, the development of abilities which may be seen in themselves as part of the educational process and which certainly will be recognized as being applicable in other kinds of learning situation. In the example we considered earlier, for instance, a good deal of learning is required not only about how one can express oneself most clearly but also why it is necessary to learn to be concise and economic in one's use of words when preparing data for feeding into the microcomputer. Précis skills are important in so many aspects of life. Important logical processes too are involved in preparing data for processing, so that there is also a major contribution here to the development of logical thinking. Nor should we ignore the educational advantages which accrue from the discovery that the microcomputer can never tell you more than you have told it, can never go beyond the data you have fed into it.

If one were to attempt to summarize this brief survey of the potential of the microcomputer in education, it would be by saying that it offers an opportunity, on a scale not previously envisaged, to direct our attention to the qualitative rather than the quantitative aspects of pupils' thinking and learning. In general terms, this is what I suggested earlier education is essentially about. The one major advantage of the microcomputer is that, if we use it properly, it offers us the best means of attaining this goal that we have yet been offered.

'Good practice'

The first point I would want to make about 'good practice' — not only in this field but everywhere — is that it must reflect clearly thought-through principles, whatever those principles are. They need not be the principles set out earlier in this chapter (although, of course, for me they will be) but there must be some underlying principles if one's practice is not to be totally random, haphazard and, possibly, as a result, incoherent. I think it was Richard Peters who once said that it is not a question of whether a teacher has a theory of education or not, it is rather whether he has a good theory of education or a bad one, a coherently worked-out theory or an unexamined and unconsidered one. This general principle is at least as relevant to the use of microcomputers as it is in any other field of education. The first criterion of good practice, then, is that it must be based on a clearly worked-out philosophy, one that has asked those important questions about *why* we propose to plan our work in certain ways.

A second and related principle, which again may have a general applicability, is that work in this area should be a genuine extension and development of what is being done elsewhere, that it should be explicable and justifiable in terms of the promotion of our general educational principles — whatever these may be — and not something merely added on without reference to its suitability and appropriateness or its relation to the rest of the curriculum provided. Merely to tack it on is, as ever, to invite disaster, for again it is to ignore the important criterion of coherence. It is the '2001' mentality which invites us to do this, but the best examples of 'good practice' in school, as subsequent chapters will reveal, are those where the teacher has not eagerly embraced the technology as a futuristic gimmick but has approached it with a proper degree of caution and asked 'How can this help me to educate my pupils?', 'How can this extend my scope and range as a teacher?', 'How can I use these machines as slaves rather than allow them to become my masters?'.

These first two principles may be regarded as largely neutral, as applicable to all or most educational developments and as acceptable whatever one's view of education is or one's principles are. Those that follow are rather more specific and by no means value-neutral, since they derive from a particular view of education and a particular set of principles. That view and those principles have already been made clear, however, so that there need be no doubt as to what is the backcloth of the points about to be made.

Perhaps the most important point that this view leads me to emphasize in this context — or, indeed, in any other — is the need for children to be actively engaged and involved in the experiences they are offered if those experiences are to satisfy this definition of education. It is not the intention here to pursue in detail the question of what such active involvement entails. That has been done elsewhere (Blenkin and Kelly 1981). It should be enough to say, first, that it is not gross physical activity that one has in mind but rather an active engagement of the intellect, a direct and real involvement with the material, and, secondly, that it is the opposite of those forms of passive learning which occur when teachers, or others, see it as their task to shovel large quantities of what Gradgrind immortalized as 'hard facts' into the supposed empty vessels of children's minds. A basic principle would, therefore, appear to be that children will gain more educational value, learn more, develop more when using the microcomputer in a positive sense, writing their own programs or at least feeding in their own data and posing their own questions, than from merely working through a second-hand program prepared for them by others, especially when those others are not only external to the school, but, as in so many cases, external to the teaching profession and thus likely to lack this kind of understanding or concept of what education in the full sense is.

The role of the teacher is, of course, crucial in this form of education and this leads us to note a second important principle. As with all educational resources, those designed for use by children on microcomputers will be far more effective if designed by teachers themselves and thus tailor-made for the context of their own pupils' learning and development. Many of the problems which we have suggested are inherent in the use of externally prepared programs begin to evaporate where these are mediated *via* the teacher, that is, when the teacher adapts them to suit his or her own purposes. They disappear altogether when the teacher prepares them himself or herself.

An interesting development of this is the use of local institutions of Further Education or Higher Education or of Secondary schools to prepare programs to particular and precise specifications. In cases where the teacher lacks the expertise — or perhaps the time — to prepare suitable material, students on computer-programming courses in other institutions can be involved. This kind of cooperation is clearly of mutual advantage to both parties, for students will make greater progress in their studies of computer programming if they have real programs to write for real situations and if they are given opportunities to observe these being used, and the pupils in the schools will have programs tailor-made to their specifications and those of their teacher. This is one interesting way in which teachers can implement this second basic principle, that pupils should, wherever possible, work with materials specially prepared with their requirements in mind.

A third principle which also derives from this concern with active learning is that the way in which the microcomputer is used should be such as to promote the development of understanding and the growth of the capacity to think rather than the mere acquisition of facts. It was the absence of this concern which characterizes much of what currently goes on in schools that prompted our earlier criticism of the use of microcomputers merely as teaching-machines. The concern is not merely with propositional knowledge, with what some have called 'knowledge *that*', nor even with procedural knowledge, called by some 'knowledge *how*', but with conceptual growth, the development of what I suppose these same people would call 'knowledge *why*'. Again this is a general principle of this view of education. Again, therefore, we must bear it in mind if our use of microcomputers is to reflect this view of education.

This, of course, constitutes another reason for eschewing the use of those externally prepared programs which children are required to work through in a largely passive manner. For these programs for the most part require a response in the form of a set answer, almost in a 'yes' or 'no' form, and thus imply that in all or most things one is either right or wrong. This approach, however, holds the pupil at the level of 'knowledge that' or, at the very best, of 'knowledge how'. The development of understanding, and indeed, of critical awareness, requires an appreciation that in most, and perhaps all, areas of human knowledge things are far more subtle and complex than that. It is important, therefore, that a pupil when interacting with a microcomputer should have constantly in mind not the question, 'Have I got it right or wrong?' but 'How can I put it right?' or 'How can I improve on what I have got?'. Again, of course, this implies a much more active role for the pupil than merely working through a program. It is what Seymour Papert (1980) has in mind, I believe, when he suggests that in using microcomputers in education we should be concerned more with qualitative than with quantitative thinking. It is a matter of encouraging the pupil to develop understanding by doing something with the knowledge he already has rather than merely to acquire more of it.

If we are to encourage this kind of activity, it is, of course, important that the pupil should feel at home with the hardware — and, indeed, as Leslie Smith stresses in Chapter 2, that the teacher should be at home with it too. This brings us to a fourth principle of 'good practice' which must be stressed. For the most probable barrier between pupil, or teacher, and this kind of familiarity of usage is the requirement to learn a complex computer language first. There are two aspects of this which must be emphasized. First, we need to note that, as subsequent chapters will show, some teachers have found it possible to develop productive uses of microcomputers without the need for the pupils to learn an elaborate computer language. One of the great advantages of LOGO is that it is simple; it enables us to talk to the microcomputer, to give it our instructions, in a language very like our own, so that children are quickly at home with it. Other computer languages can also be used in a much more simplified form than most of the basic manuals would seem to suggest, especially if the teacher recognizes the need to simplify the process for the pupils as far as is possible.

The second aspect of this issue is perhaps even more important. For we should make it a principle that, even if we feel the need for our pupils to learn a computer language, they should learn it by using it, that we should not provide them with a computer-language course first and only let them use it when we believe they have achieved a degree of proficiency in it. Again this is a principle which is applicable to all learning of so-called 'basic skills', whether these be the 'skills' of reading, of writing, of calculating or even of working in wood or metal or some other material. To teach the 'skills' in isolation from their use is, firstly, to teach them inefficiently, secondly, to make the subsequent learning of how to use them more difficult, and thirdly, and most crucially, to invite a rejection of them prompted by the boredom of repetition and irrelevant exercises. If parents taught their young children to talk in the way that many of them are subsequently taught to read or to write, society would have another kind of literacy problem. We all learn most efficiently, most effectively and, above all, most committedly by doing and, indeed, by doing things we can see a point or purpose to. This principle is at least as crucial to the use of microcomputers in education as to any other kind of learning. Thus to sit pupils or students in rows and teach them how to use a microcomputer by *telling* them seems to me quite unforgivable. It is almost as unforgivable, however, even by more sophisticated methods, to set out to teach them a computer language first. Using a skill productively is always a better way of acquiring and then of honing it. This is another fundamental principle of active learning.

A further principle of 'good practice' that needs to be borne in mind is one which has already been touched on. For mention was made, in listing the potential dangers of using microcomputers merely as teaching machines, of the particular problem of solitary forms of learning. It is probably necessary for all pupils at certain stages to be locked into some kind of solitary communion with a microcomputer. Indeed, there is a fundamental sense in which all learning is at heart a solitary activity. However, reference was made earlier to recent claims for the importance of the social dimension of learning. There are at least two sides to this. One is the evidence of recent studies that children actually learn better when their teachers take steps to create a suitably reassuring social climate in which they can work. The second is that social and moral dimension of eduction, to which reference was also made earlier in this chapter. For, if we accept that this is important, if we believe that to have been educated is to have developed socially and morally as well as intellectually, then we must look to the implications for that kind of development in all that we do as teachers. In relation to the use of microcomputers, then, we must monitor carefully the kinds of use of them made by pupils from this point of view. For, as was suggested earlier, to ignore this aspect is to take a step towards that society, depicted by E.M. Forster, in which all social contact between individuals has disappeared or at least has been reduced to the kind of second-order intercourse which is conducted through the various products of technological development.

Reference to the moral and social dimension of education brings me to the last point I wish to make in this attempt to set out the basic principles of 'good practice'. It is important that, in the way in which we use the microcomputer, we encourage pupils to recognize it as a tool for them to use and thus to see its role in society as a tool for mankind to use — as a slave and not as a master. For, as with all technological developments, there are real dangers if micro-chip technology is misused by society, or if there is not proper thought and concern for how it is to be used. Much of what has been said about the need for teachers to think carefully about its use in education can be extended to the need for us all to consider very carefully its use in society as a whole. Already, on two occasions, reference has been made to Forster's *The Machine Stops*. One of the warnings offered by that book, and, indeed, by Orwell's *1984* and Huxley's *Brave New World*, is that if technological advance is misused it can have disastrous social consequences. Mention was also made earlier of the inevitability with which social change follows technological development. This is not, however, a simple matter of cause and effect; what kind of social change occurs depends entirely on how mankind uses that technological development. The kind of social change that is engendered by the micro-chip, then, will depend on how we use that particular kind of technological expertise.

It is for this reason that we must give a good deal of thought to how we use it in schools. And it is for this reason that one of the things we must do in schools is to encourage pupils not merely to accept it nor merely to use it, in whatever sophisticated ways we can devise, but also, and crucially, to consider its uses, both in school and in society, in a properly critical and analytical way. It is important, then, particularly for older pupils, although we should not underrate the capacity of young children for sensible exploration of such issues, that the moral and social implications of the computer-age be carefully and thoroughly aired and considered.

The political implications of this development are immense. There are already signs, some of which appear in what has been said earlier in this chapter, of movement towards *1984*, towards the society depicted by Forster, towards a world which is far from brave — the devaluing of the Humanities in our curricula, not only in schools but also in Higher Education, a corresponding weakening of the arts in society, a preference for economic rather than humanitarian criteria in the making of political decisions, a general social and moral malaise. The only defence against this is a society of people whose education has led them to be properly critical, deeply thoughtful and capable of making informed choices rather than merely responding to passing whims and fancies. It is for this reason, more than any other, that 'good practice' is crucial, not only in the use of microcomputers in schools, but right across the school curriculum.

Summary and conclusions

This chapter has set out to persuade the reader that the present use of microcomputers in schools leaves much to be desired and, indeed, offers some things to be deplored. It has suggested that there are two aspects to this problem; first, the dangers inherent in certain kinds of misuse and, second, the sad loss of the educational potential this development seems to offer. An attempt was then made to identify the major features of that potential, particularly when it is considered in the context of a view of education as a multi-faceted form of human development. Finally, in the light of that discussion, certain principles of what might constitute 'good practice' in this field were set out and the conclusion was reached that these principles might well be important not only for the development of individual children, nor even just for that of education, but also for the development of society itself.

How far these principles can be translated into such 'good practice' will, of course, like all else in education, depend crucially on the quality of teachers and specifically on their understanding not only of the technology but especially of the educational potential of the microcomputer. Subsequent chapters will reveal what some teachers can do and are doing on the basis of that kind of expertise. First, however, we must recognize that these represent a very small proportion of the country's teaching force. For the rest, a real effort must soon be made not only to make them aware of the potential which this chapter has attempted to describe but also to overcome the natural reluctance many of them feel to expose themselves to a development of which they are not only ignorant but also apprehensive. It is to this problem that we turn in Chapter 2.

CHAPTER 2

OVERCOMING COMPUTER-INDUCED ANXIETY

LESLIE A. SMITH

This chapter reflects the fact that teachers and pre-service students will have to face up to the need to gain a familiarity with computers as they work with their pupils in the contemporary classroom. The 'future' of five years ago arrived last year: the 'future' that lies ahead can only intensify the need for teacher-involvement in at least microcomputer operations if not the whole range of Information Technology of which the microcomputer is a significant part.

This poses a number of problems for teachers irrespective of the age group of pupils they teach or will teach. One of these problems comes to us in a familiar guise — curriculum innovation with all that this implies to the class-based teacher. Another problem is more specific inasmuch as it concerns a particular form of anxiety which might add its weight to the more general emotions associated with curriculum innovation; and I have called this 'computer-induced anxiety' for ease of reference rather than anything else.

I am on safe ground using the term 'anxiety' because it is in the realm of common experience, but by linking it causally with the term 'computer-induced' I expect to be challenged. Fair enough. The point I am trying to make is that the prospect of sitting at a microcomputer keying-in a series of commands seems to arouse a number of complex emotions among some teachers, and there is ample evidence to suggest that some people not only lack confidence when confronted by a microcomputer but react in an anxious manner sometimes to the point where they 'turn-off'. They have my sympathy and, hopefully, should they read this chapter, my support. Because of the need to involve all teachers in a computer-literacy programme, I feel that somebody should attempt to turn empathy into words so that those teachers who doubt their ability to cope with microcomputers might find some support and guidance which will put things in perspective.

This is the aim of my chapter. I have divided it into two sections, one dealing with some of the ingredients of 'self-doubt' and the other presenting some suggestions for a 'self-help' approach for those teachers who have yet to enjoy the experience of being 'hands-on' with a microcomputer.

Self-doubt

This section looks at a few of the problems facing the computer-novice teacher. It is offered in the belief that to describe a problem is a step towards understanding it, and that to understand a problem is a first step towards solving it.

Information Technology and the curriculum

Pressures are building up for the inclusion (or extension) of at least selected aspects of Information Technology in the curriculum of the school be it Infant, Junior or Secondary. The main thrust of this curriculum lobby is coming from the various industries which are engaged in the development of Information Technology; but there is no doubt that the education service itself is developing a rapidly acquired interest in this relatively recently named area of human activity. The government has added its weight to the introduction of a Computer Literacy Programme in schools both through wordy encouragement and financial aid in the form of gifts of microcomputers to schools in the maintained sector. Things are on the move as teachers gain support from the Inspectorate (HMI), the Local Advisory Service, and institutions charged with the task of educating and training pre-service teachers.

This should come as no surprise. Information Technology, as we noted in Chapter 1, embraces a large number of features of contemporary life and, unlike some areas of technological advance, it is apparent that it is having a widespread impact on the general public. Furthermore, Information Technology is currently enjoying a rapid rate of development, particularly in the fields of television and computer science.

Television is about to 'take-off' yet again with the advent of cable television and, perhaps more important, direct satellite television. Teletext services have enjoyed rapid development with Britain leading Europe in the number of users. Prestel, perhaps the most exciting of these, is developing links with home-based microcomputers so creating the potential of dialogue between the two. Teletext 'Yellow Pages' using regionally based centres and cable links or home-based microcomputer/cable links are developments which are not far away. The same is true of 'teleshopping' and cable/microcomputer shopping in selected parts of the retail trade — an extension of existing developments in the wholesale trade. The field of visual communications has been on the boil for some years, and graphics, particularly computer graphics, have become a feature of our lives. Mainframe computers with their satellite terminals and free-standing or linked microcomputers are transforming information retrieval, uses of information, and ways of handling an ever-increasing amount and range of information. Question-posing is a growing skill which has been developed by people using computers of all types, and this skill now joins problem-solving in the lives of owners of microcomputers. International communications are taking giant strides forward as the satellites in geosynchronous orbit (allocated to the world's nations on paper in 1977) take their places 23,000 miles above the earth's surface; and these equatorially orbiting satellites will also bring us the direct satellite television mentioned earlier.

These events poised to take place in the next few years are but a sample of the developments taking place in the field of Information Technology. It is an exciting world-wide development we are witnessing, and at the heart of this is the microcomputer with its versatility already proved. In the United Kingdom alone, more than two million homes will possess a microcomputer by the time this book is published. Think for a moment of how these developments will be taken as 'given' by children who are born today and who will join us in school five years hence. Children inherit past inventions: they start where we find amazement; they expect us to be familiar with the world they can explore uncluttered by previously acquired inhibitions. The opportunities for children being involved early in their lives with microcomputers are increasing daily; and as they grow older the chances of their coming face to face with the keyboard of a microcomputer will also increase rapidly. They, the future children, and the children already in school pose us an additional series of problems as their thirst for computer literacy is initially promoted and later satisfied by teachers who have found the skills to explore with them this relatively new world of communications.

This may sound dramatic, even unbelievable. After all, we are still grappling with the problems of orthodox literacy and numeracy when we work with our pupils, and it is quite easy to dismiss the notion of computer literacy as a fringe benefit for children from middle-class families whose parents are more likely to own a home computer than other adults in the population. But this does not change the fact that the participatory ingredient to be found in the new information technology is itself new. In earlier times, developments in radio and then television put the listening and viewing audiences in a passive stance, and this remains true of much 'information' which is broadcast by these media. The microcomputer is changing this image of applied information technology. Today's environment contains enough visible evidence to suggest that we cannot wait for even more dramatic changes to take place before we consider most seriously the inclusion in the curriculum of selected aspects of the practical applications of a rapidly developing information technology. This is where we are in education. Hopefully, these developments will be viewed as a motivating challenge to teachers, all teachers, in spite of the fact that they also make a significant challenge to our existing priorities in and attitudes towards educational practice. Certainly, it would appear that we cannot leave the development of school-based programmes of (a) Information Studies and (b) Computer Literacy to a few enthusiasts, and certainly not to outside agencies. We are all involved.

Microcomputers and curriculum development

It is not my job to convince teachers that there is an inevitability about their eventual involvement with information studies and computer literacy: the passage of time itself will accomplish this. I am more concerned with the effects that this will have on some teachers! The pressures on teachers who are being asked to become involved will increase; and as a concomitant of this it is likely that there will be some teachers who view such developments as threats to their security, as causes of anxiety. This is not a new phenomenon reserved solely for the microcomputer: all forms of curriculum innovation are likely to create tensions among the staff of a school. But it must be said that unless something is done quickly, the types of development in school which centre round the microcomputer are likely to be stuck in a model of curriculum development which has a poor track record as far as the classroom-based teacher is concerned. I refer to the model labelled 'centre/periphery model of curriculum innovation'.

Many of the curriculum development projects which are based on the centre/periphery model will be familiar to you, if only as names you have heard. Projects in the fields of science and mathematics financed by the Nuffield Foundation in the 1950s and 1960s and most of the early projects funded by the Schools Council in the 1960s and early 1970s involved centrally based developmental teams who worked to provide materials for use in schools, particularly Junior and Secondary schools. They served a purpose at the time by highlighting the need for curriculum innovation in important areas of school-based education; though the model itself came under criticism because the gap between the central team and the teachers in the classroom proved to be difficult to bridge, with the result that the take-up of the projects by teachers was haphazard, generally poor, and heavily reliant on the existence of a school-based enthusiasm which was difficult to foster. Even when enthusiasm among teachers of a school brought the centrally produced project into the on-going debate about the nature of the curriculum of the school concerned, lack of funds to acquire the project's resources for learning and/or the lack of expertise among the staff often forced the school to abandon its provisional plans to absorb the project into its curriculum. There were also cases in which a centrally produced curriculum project was technically taken up by a school, which then proceeded to misinterpret the originating team's array of ideas with disastrous consequences both for the school and for the reputation of the project concerned.

The Schools Council, goaded by the failure of the centre/periphery model to create change in schools in a significant manner, studied the problem at a crucial meeting at Worthing in 1972, and thereafter included the concept of dissemination into its existing and future projects. Later, the central staff of the Schools Council discovered another truth: even a general understanding of the process of dissemination points to the vital need to make direct contact with individual teachers so that the process replicates the general educational process to be found in the effective classroom, i.e. the one-to-one dialogue, the availability of support when it is needed, the genuine sharing of understanding which leads to educational development and growth. We also know that this is very difficult to achieve.

Thus, to the extent that programmes involving the use of microcomputers in a school setting are externally produced and rely for take-up on the enthusiasm of a few teachers in a school, then we must expect a rather ragged response from a significant number of teachers. Admittedly, the dissemination process has been employed with enthusiasm by developmental teams, and coverage afforded to the key programme 'computer literacy' has been most efficient. For example, the BBC's series of ten television programmes, broadcast in early 1982 and repeated twice in 1983, have done a great deal to alert teachers to the potential of a computer-literacy programme in school and have offered them a gentle introduction to microcomputing.

But a great deal remains to be done to allay any anxiety a computer-novice teacher may have as he/she faces up to a 'hands-on' experience with a computer keyboard; and even more remains to be done to ensure that teachers who have gained computer experience develop critical powers so that they may evaluate commercially produced computer programs against those educationally orientated criteria which we discussed in Chapter 1. The teacher needs time: time to adjust, time to learn, time to develop personal ideas about the ways the microcomputer may be used to assist in the learning situation of the classroom. Unfortunately, we are being overtaken by events.

Take the case of the one-off gift of a microcomputer by the government to each school. There sits the equipment. It presents a challenge or poses a threat depending on the teacher's point of view. To be realistic, we should admit to ourselves that we have got to make the effort to put the machine to good use. It is no longer a question of being motivated to learn about something new because inner feelings promote the urge so to do. The microcomputer 'gift' is difficult to ignore. Therefore an element of compulsion has entered the centre/periphery model of curriculum innovation, and experience has shown that this is often counter-productive in terms of aimed-for teacher participation. Furthermore, it will soon be found that one microcomputer will not meet all the needs of the school, and teachers will have to become involved in decision-making in curricular terms as more machines are considered for acquisition and use in school.

Computers and anxiety

The pressures referred to in the previous two sections might not be immediately apparent to all teachers on the staff of any given school. Even when they are perceived to exist, reaction to them will produce different results depending on the attitudes of the teachers concerned and the age group of pupils for whom they have responsibility. For example, a Secondary school which long ago became involved in microcomputing (or computer studies which relied upon the use of external mainframe computers) might have seen this activity as a natural extension of the work of the mathematics department; and it is quite likely that where this is the case, the same department will be expected to continue its role as custodian of the stock of microcomputers while enlarging its field of operations to embrace areas of the curriculum

additional to computer studies. Such an approach to a broadening of the base of computer literacy might face a number of difficulties which derive from the departmentalization of the Secondary school curriculum; and the mathematics department, or any department charged with responsibility for the school's computers (e.g. science), will have to sponsor and react to the need for collaboration with the other departments of the school, not all of whom will see the point of becoming involved.

This is an age-old problem in the Secondary school as is shown by the various attempts that have been made over the years to promote variations on the theme of integrated studies without a great deal of success. But within the structure of a subject-based curriculum, it is highly likely that the tendency to centralize the siting and overall control of the stock of microcomputers will act as a brake on universal participation by the teaching staff of the school unless exceptional steps are taken to avoid this natural phenomenon; or, put another way, it will provide a first-class excuse for teachers who have little contact with the department concerned to avoid involvement with the school's microcomputing programme, unless they are encouraged to view the computer literacy programme in a 'new' light.

The logistic solution to this educational problem seems to involve either the creation of a computer centre on 'neutral ground' (like the creation of capital cities of nations which embrace the federal system) *or* the more expensive creation of a decentralized system in which designated teaching areas are equipped with their own free-standing microcomputers *or* a really expensive combination of both of these strategies (as might be seen in the existence and use of both a central library and classroom libraries). Certainly, in terms of the availability of microcomputers in sufficient number to offer hands-on experience to most if not all pupils, the Secondary school is better placed than its Primary school counterparts to become involved in an updated version of a computer literacy programme which will enjoy the participation of most if not all members of the staff.

The Primary sector of education, traditionally divided into Infant and Junior schools but now embracing a number of combinations of schools catering for the age group 5 to 13, faces a different set of problems. Few of these schools possess 'departments' which historically controlled microcomputer operations in the school; in fact, few of these schools have created departments in the style of their Secondary school counterparts. More to the point, until recently few of these schools owned a microcomputer or had access to a microcomputer. But now things are changing. The Primary sector is being equipped slowly with the means to engage in a programme of computer literacy which will involve young children gaining the vital hands-on experience that this programme demands. As more and more equipment arrives in the school, the opportunities for a most effective engagement in this computer programme increase dramatically; and the previous lack of resources produces a situation in which the Primary school can view the programme with an exciting freshness, uncluttered by previously created practices.

Having said that, I feel that it is important that the Primary school, viewing its perhaps solitary microcomputer, should not start its practical involvement with microcomputers by handing custody of the machine (except for storage) to one member of its staff without ensuring that a programme of shared use is both created and implemented. The Secondary school might have problems, related to departmentalism and an early start in teaching computer studies, which reflect an unavoidable accident of 'history' and which might create impediments to the involvement in the computer literacy programme of all members of the staff; but there is no reason why this particular historical obstacle should be created in the Primary school. It may be naive to refer to the long history of 'sharing and caring' which the Primary sector of education in Britain is supposed to enjoy. However, I believe that this is true not only because of sentiment based on observations but because of an understanding of the ways in which small groups of teachers, the staffs of school-units, are likely to work together; but I feel that the nature of this particular brand of group work is such that it will help the Primary school gain a quality of teacher involvement in the computer literacy programme which will provide lessons for those of us engaged in other sectors of the education service.

Nobody in education can doubt the existence among some teachers and pupils of an enthusiasm for microcomputing; however, it is doubtful if this is evenly spread so that each school has its quota of existing enthusiasm for this relatively new activity in schools of all types. From what we know of the centre/periphery model of curriculum innovation, it is a necessary ingredient of school-based innovation for somebody on the staff to possess a degree of enthusiasm for the new educational programme concerned. How this can be achieved in each school so that the take-up of the computer literacy programme is universal, if tentatively so? One would hope that the headteacher is alert to the pressure being exerted on the curriculum of his/her school for the inclusion of this programme as a matter of some urgency; but, again, experience of curriculum innovation shows that the headteacher (and other members of the school leadership) needs support from other classroom-based teachers if the take-up is to become effective.

We can continue asking this hypothetical question about take-up of microcomputing until we reach a situation where the answers reveal not so much a general lack of enthusiasm among the staff of a school but rather a general nervousness about being able to cope with microcomputing. This is a very real and serious problem.

There are many factors which singly or together might cause a teacher to view the prospect of operating a microcomputer with a degree of nervousness, apprehension and anxiety, some of which derive from the process of curriculum innovation. But curriculum innovation apart, there are some factors which centre on microcomputing itself. I would like to describe briefly some of these.

Firstly, there is the air of mystery about the work carried out by systems analysts, programmers and operaters of mainframe computers, which derives from the early days of electronic computing but which has not been dispelled as five generations of computers have emerged from the creative skills of computer technologists. Some older teachers will remember the ways in which people with scientific leanings and/or mathematical talents were sought-after by the computer industry; and both computer technologists and computer operators were viewed as being people blessed with 'special talents'. All teachers will know that computer people, past and present, have left a trail of jargon (no doubt technically necessary) and a shorthand type of logic which when turned into a printed program seems to make sense to the initiated few but remains a coded message to the uninitiated many.

It is against this backcloth that teachers are being asked to place aside any preconceptions they might have about the talents needed to be a computer operator so that they may be encouraged by a very enthusiastic computer industry to take microcomputing seriously. Some teachers will find this difficult to do. They will have long-since made the self-assessment of their own interests, learning styles, strengths and natural penchant, and having matched this assessment against what they perceive (rightly or wrongly) to be the talents needed to be a successful computer programmer or operator, they will have concluded that microcomputing is simply 'not their scene'. Who can blame them for such a view? To some extent it has been created by the same computer industry which now courts their interest and involvement.

Secondly, there is a feeling commonly expressed by the computer novice that their exposure to the keyboard of a microcomputer will make them look foolish as they fumble with keys carrying symbols some of which they do not immediately comprehend. There are dozens of reasons why people feel this way: most of them are psychologically based. The key word seems to be 'look' in 'look foolish'. The question to be answered is 'Who is watching?'; and if this doesn't help resolve the problem, then a more important question should be asked; 'Does it really matter if you do look and feel foolish?' Thankfully, this problem is short-lived if it is handled with true empathy by those who are able to help a 'look foolish' computer novice. But it should be emphasized that the quality of the help needed by people who feel this way is a crucial factor in effecting a cure: it must not be patronizing, it must not be rushed and couched in jargon, it must reflect a genuine understanding of the need for an undamaged ego to emerge from the experience.

Thirdly, there is a factor related to the 'look foolish' syndrome. This is more difficult to handle because it reflects a microcomputer-novice teacher's reactions to a situation in which young children seem to possess more confidence, more knowledge, more skill than the teacher concerned. A 'does it really matter?' approach to this teacher-felt problem cuts no ice. The problem is more deep-seated in the attitude of the teacher and the ways he/she sees his/her role in the classroom. Few teachers would even admit that such a problem exists for them or for other teachers. But it has to be faced, even if it is a problem which worries only a very few teachers. My reason for stressing this point is that a crystal ball is not needed to forecast that in Infant, Junior and Secondary schools there will be pupils who have enjoyed home-based microcomputing with their parents, brothers and sisters, and peers, and who will bring to school microcomputing skills and knowledge which will be equal, if not superior, to those possessed by many of their teachers. Therefore, a teacher who is worried about being less knowledgeable and/or less skilled in microcomputing than some of his/her pupils is likely to find so many instances when this will really be true that he/she will have to accept not only the reality of the situation but also the educational advantages such a situation possesses, no matter how difficult they are to discern.

Fourthly, the computer-novice teacher might well share space in a school with colleagues who have made a start in the process of gaining microcomputer expertise. The *real* expert in microcomputing will understand the special needs of the novice: the 'expert-in-the-making' may not enjoy such a degree of mastery over microcomputing that such special needs cannot be (a) remembered from past experience and (b) dealt with in an understanding manner. To be blunt; too many pseudo-casual, off-hand, rapidly executed demonstrations of what are really recently acquired skills, might prove something to the demonstrator/counsellor whose help has been sought, but they do absolutely nothing for the novice . . . except, perhaps, reinforce beliefs about personal inadequacy. The computer novice should remember this when it is his/her turn to help others.

Fifthly, there is no escaping from the fact that the microcomputer is a marvel of human ingenuity and, at least initially, a complicated machine to operate properly. This is recognized by the manufacturers (in spite of some aspects of the sales-promotion drive currently in evidence), as comments in the introductory literature illustrate. For example, the literature accompanying the BBC Microcomputer (Acorn B) informs first-time users: 'Don't worry if you make a mistake . . . it really doesn't matter'; and, 'If you are a keyboard "novice" you may find the layout daunting. Don't worry — first of all it is not necessary to be a touch typist to work the computer . . .' (Coll and Allen 1982, pp.10 and 15). 'Learning these [instructions to the microcomputer] is like riding a bicycle — maybe you'll take a bit of a time to get the hang of things but persevere and you'll soon get enormous satisfaction from owning this machine. You will slowly find more and more things it can do' (Allen 1981, p.3).

Statements like these would not appear in introductory handbooks without good reason. They offer sound advice even if the novice finds them slightly off-putting. The truth is that within the time-span needed for the novice to gain up to twenty hours 'hands-on' experience with a microcomputer keyboard, it will become clear to this person that microcomputing is an activity which requires concentration, not a little skill in using a keyboard albeit with mostly one and occasionally two hands (or one finger on each hand), an appreciation that the keyboard is to some extent similar to the keyboard of an *electric* typewriter (not the manual machine), an eye for detail as programs are keyed-in, a real appreciation of one's own learning processes, and above all a sense of great satisfaction as one gains confidence and makes ready to design one's own first program — "MYPROG1".

Finally, there is the crucial matter of the pace of learning that is involved when approaching microcomputing, both initially and subsequently. If anything, the machine is more like a musical instrument than a bicycle and we are all rather impatient with our progress; with the result that there is a tendency for frustration to figure prominently in our learning. To continue the analogy with the musical instrument: practising the scale exercises is a prerequisite for eventually playing a tune; and practising keying-in the components of program exercises is a forerunner to eventually writing "MYPROG1". If anything, the failure to accept a reasonable pace of learning is the key to much that might be called 'computer-induced anxiety'. In reality, it's got nothing to do with the microcomputer: it's the anxious learner bringing his/her previously acquired problems to the machine which is the factor most involved in the self-doubt I have tried to describe in this section.

Self-help

This section of my chapter emphasizes the fact that microcomputing, like so many activities, is best learned through physical contact with a microcomputer. Such contact, known as 'hands-on' (the keyboard, that is!), can be enjoyed solo, in collaboration with one or more people, or in a class setting, though the last is not as profitable as the other two. Experience has shown that adults need up to twenty hours hands-on experience to obtain a degree of mastery over the operations of a microcomputer so that the road to personally devised programs may be opened. This is a generalization, of course, but twenty hours' experience is quite a long time in terms of powers of concentration, and it is recommended that they be spread over a period of weeks rather than days so that the process of learning may be given a chance to work effectively. To be sure, it is a process which cannot be rushed.

Teachers in schools might like to know that pre-service students — at least those on the longer, concurrent courses — will henceforth receive at least twenty hours' experience with microcomputers as part of their professional studies course at college or university. It is from the planning and operating of such activities with pre-service and in-service teachers that this 'self-help' section has emerged. Those of us involved with this programme at one college have discovered no particular secrets as we search for ways to help students towards computer literacy; but we have been able to sift through previous experience with students to find techniques which seem to offer some hope of quick success.

The first and most important of these relates to an individualized approach to teaching/learning. Microcomputing is a skill which is within the capabilities of most literate people, but each individual learns about it in different ways and at a different pace, and this must be taken into account when we are offering or receiving computer experience. However, as I hope to demonstrate, there is a strong case to be made for pair or small-group activity in which individuals are able to share their 'solo' experience with others. Such sharing is at the heart of any self-help process, for 'self-help' in this context does not mean 'teach yourself without external help'. In fact, the secret of learning seems to involve the ability to (a) know when help is needed, (b) articulate the questions that need to be asked to gain the needed help, and (c) find the agency and/or person who is most likely to understand the questions and provide necessary guidance.

Keyboard experience

The introductory manuals and cassettes which accompany most keyboard-type microcomputers offer both guidance and facilities for practice on the keyboard. The BBC WELCOME cassette contains an excellent program for keyboard practice and its regular use is to be recommended at the start of each keyboard session, at least for the first few hours of experience. Such programs can be augmented by a pairing process in which one person sits at the keyboard while the other calls out symbols (taken from a keyboard diagram or another keyboard) to be keyed in. In this way, some of the necessary keyboard symbolism is put into words, rehearsed as such while being related to the actual symbols to be found on the keyboard, and generally committed to memory by the two people involved in the exercises.

It will be realized quite quickly that the electronic keyboard requires the lightest of touch as each symbol-key is pressed, and, as the literature states, you do not have to be a touch-typist to key-in accurately and effectively. The thing to watch is the upper-case and lower-case position of some symbols, the upper-case ones requiring the use of the shift key to bring them into operation. The same problem exists when a key has been given multiple functions on machines which do not closely resemble the keyboard of an electric typewriter.

Initially, the 'special' keys, e.g. the red keys of a BBC Acorn B microcomputer, can be ignored, but they come into their own as the novice gets to grips with the concept of allocating a special meaning to a given symbol, and realizes that, while some symbols have been allocated to special functions, it remains a fact that the operator has the power to give meaning to almost any symbol. In this respect, the process is similar to that to be found in algebra.

The fun thing about the keyboard is the process of editing the message you have typed into a line. Modern and expensive electric typewriters have provided the typist with similar facilities for some time, but most of us who try to type have suffered the frustration of keying-in as many errors as are to be found in contemporary newpapers. The microcomputer enables the operator to delete errors and make good any repairs. You will get a lot of practice doing this.

The user guide

Personally, I find these more off-putting than the microcomputer itself. They are not a 'good read', but then, they have not been produced for this purpose.

Apart from the introductory section, which can be read before keyboard experience is enjoyed for too long, the user guide is a resource to be used when (a) problems arise and (b) next steps need to be taken.

I can appreciate the problems facing those people who write these guides: the complex nature of microcomputing makes it necessary for them to offer guidance under specific headings. But this form of presentation is not always helpful to the novice who is unlikely to be able to name the area in which help is sought until he/she has enjoyed several hours of keyboard experience, or even programming experience. To enable the novice to gain the most help from the user guide, I recommend that he/she is encouraged to maintain a log or diary of the work done on the keyboard. Such a log should indicate the nature of any problem encountered and the page reference of the user guide which describes both the problem and its solution. Initially, the novice will find that it will take some time to flash-read through the guide to find the relevant section for each problem that arises (the experience is not unlike that of trying to find a telephone number via Yellow Pages), and although this is an education in itself, it can be a boring part of microcomputing. By noting the problem and the solution and the page reference of the guide concerned, the novice will find that the learning process is made less frustrating.

Handling the equipment

There will be enough warning labels placed on the various pieces of equipment to inform the user about the need to wire-up components correctly and earth the hardware in the proper manner. Take heed of these notices and warnings. But have you noticed the tendency for manufacturers to urge you to consult an expert should you be in doubt? This is very proper in terms of safety; but it also points to a vital part of the learning process which involves the learner seeking help when self-proposed solutions to a problem seem to fail. The point I am making is that we tend to have no qualms about calling for help when the gadgets go wrong (even when the called-for technician solves our problems by switching on the electricity!), or when our safety is at stake, but we seem to be reluctant to call for help for a problem which we think we should solve ourselves. The microcomputer novice should view keyboard operations as being fraught with frustration, anxiety-promoting, a hazard to health! Call for help once you have tried to solve a problem without success.

To return to the equipment, I feel that the novice needs to practise handling the hardware and software under supervision until he/she can cope alone.

This is an essential part of the training needed by a teacher who will be responsible for the equipment when it is being used by children.

Thankfully, the microcomputer tends to be a robust machine; but the leads joining a cassette-player or disc drive to the microcomputer are, like the cassette-player, cassette or disc drive and disc, points of weakness which must be cared for and regularly checked. There is nothing more frustrating than to have the visual display unit show 'Block?' or 'Data?' and 'Rewind tape' as the microcomputer tries to make sense of messages being sent to it via faulty equipment. (A polite note to manufacturers: look into this problem, please. The microcomputer novice and classroom teacher have enough to contend with without having to attach self-blame to what is often malfunctioning software and associated equipment.)

Pair-work and group-work

I have given one example of the way pair-work can be used by novices, and both pair-work and small group-work are essential aspects of microcomputing, both at the start and thereafter. This sharing of confidence, of ideas, of experience, of knowledge, in a natural manner is the basis upon which solo-work can be carried out effectively. For the novice, shared-help is an activity which is most successful when it emerges almost by chance as the solo-operator starts to wrestle with a problem; and the skilled teacher will know how to engineer such shared-help through 'chance' encounters rather than appear to be hovering and telegraphing an expectation that problems are on their way.

Machine-operating skills can be shared by group-work of this type; but the deliberate use of group-sharing really comes into its own when programming is under discussion. The initial group-discussion to (a) isolate a task for the computer, (b) analyse the component parts of the many problems involved in this task, (c) develop the ingredients of a tentative program, (d) evaluate this program through critical analysis almost as if the 'debugging' stage has been reached, is of great help to the novice programmer as well as to those with more expertise. Experience has shown that the task to be set the computer is likely to promote real learning experience in programming if the task itself is 'real', i.e. has meaning when the input and output of the microcomputer (and its supportive humans) are dealing with real-life situations rather than artificial exercises. This seems to be true of so many experiences we enjoy in education.

Summary and conclusions

In this chapter, I have tried to present a number of situations in the realm of contemporary educational practice in which the teacher with little or no experience of microcomputers might find himself/herself. If one of the situations I have described is seen by one teacher to be relevant, pertinent, then the chapter will have served some use. At a more theoretical level, the chapter offers a view of the type of empathy that is needed if we are to help people with justifiable anxieties face up to the problems involved and, perhaps, overcome them. I would simply add that children are people too. They, too, might have 'hang-ups' which need careful handling as they join us on the exciting journey that leads to computer literacy.

CHAPTER 3

COMPUTERS IN THE PRIMARY CLASSROOM

DAVID DODDS

Malpractice

In silicon the educational alchemists had discovered their philosopher's stone, and the software that they produced from their retorts in the mid 1970s and early 1980s revealed that once again alchemy was failing.

5 × 3 = ? said the flashing cursor
Close procedure
Fill in the missing verb

Fools' gold! The pseudo-scientists did not realize that they had fitted their lenses the wrong way round in the MICROscopes. They were looking from the microcomputer into the classroom, instead of looking from the vantage point of the classroom. The computer was not in the hands of prophets and pioneers; unfortunately it was in the hands of profiteers and pretenders. Of their wares T.E.S. said (Taylor 1982):

> It seems that most of this software has been written by programmers who know little about education, by educators who are not proficient programmers, and by opportunists who have sufficient expertise in neither programming nor education.

Many of these software producers saw the micro either as an 'improved-model' programmed learning machine, or as an 'electronic flash card cum test-and-score machine'. Of the former this had been said some ten years earlier:

It is an abiding irony of the newer media that despite their ability to revolutionize and upgrade the quality of education they can by the same token prolong and mirror what is already going on in school. Programmed instruction is a very useful and efficient way of dumping more information into children's heads. Computer-assisted instruction may actually *increase* the amount of drill and practice in the classroom. (Hooper 1971a, p.413)

Of the latter, a conference on Micros in the Classroom held in Croydon in October 1982 concluded (Stevens 1982):

Plans to put a computer into every primary school within two years could set primary education back 20 years . . . machines will be flooded into schools long before teachers have been trained to use them and before the educational computer programs they will need have been written . . . Faced with a machine they know little about, teachers could be tempted to opt for a simple 'practice and drill' programs, mainly produced for an eager market of anxious parents . . . . . 'Eighty percent of the programs available are garbage', the Inner London Education Authority's adviser said, 'They're real education dinosaurs'.

It is ironic that one of the technical terms used to describe the television screen atop a micro is a 'monitor'. The last time monitors were introduced into the classroom was in the early eighteen hundreds by Lancaster and Bell — the famous monitorial system, the aim of which was to enable rote learning and testing to take place in the absence of the qualified teacher.

Put back the clock twenty years? Nearly two hundred years would be nearer the truth!

Those who would introduce the computer into the Primary classroom should look first at the classroom, and then at the computer to see what contribution it can make.

The first major report on education published since the introduction of the microcomputer has been Cockcroft (DES 1982). On the contribution of the microcomputer it said 'The fundamental criterion at all stages must be the extent to which any piece of software offers opportunity to enhance and improve work in the classroom' (op.cit. p.119). For at a time of diminishing educational resources the computer — if it does not enrich, enhance and improve Primary classroom practice — is a very expensive artefact, and doubly so if it actually detracts from good practice.

There are currently a number of programs on the market aimed at introducing 'number' to Infants. These will utilize good high-resolution graphics to 'draw' items such as trees, oranges and yachts, and the child will then be invited to input the number of items displayed. (Perhaps the worst of these programs then continues by inviting the child to add together unlike sets — to the oranges add the houses!) Those who purvey these programs obviously have not considered that sound Infant method states that young children learn by actually handling and manipulating the 'real' artefact. Those who purchase the program have not stopped to consider the relative costs involved — a set of plastic counting apparatus versus a computer plus a cassette plus a colour monitor plus a program. As Jeff Taylor (1982) has said, 'The evaluator must take great care not to be so dazzled by the technical virtuosity of the medium that she or he cannot see just what is being taught'.

'Good Primary practice'

Cockcroft in his report 'Mathematics Counts' (DES 1982) said of the computer that it must enhance and improve work in the classroom. Therefore our starting point on any discussion on computers in the Primary classroom should be the classroom itself. Having set our 'frame of reference' we are then in a position to look at the contribution that a computer might make to classroom practice.

Chapter 1 attempted to identify what might generally constitute 'good practice' in the use of microcomputers in the classroom. One of the points made there too was that the microcomputer should be used only as a tool for extending the scope of our educational ambitions. It is important, therefore, to begin a discussion of the use of microcomputers in the Primary school by attempting to define 'good Primary practice'.

What constitutes 'good Primary practice' can be argued. However, if we investigate authoritative literature over the time-span of English Primary education then certain elements that contribute to 'good practice' can be identified and extracted, and these will be seen to relate to those general educational principles set out in Chapter 1.

Perhaps some selected quotations from the major official publications on Primary education will suffice to outline the main features of our view of 'good practice'.

The Hadow Report (1931)

'Hitherto the general tendency has been to take for granted the existence of certain traditional "subjects" and to present them to the pupils as lessons to be mastered. There is, as we have said, a place for that method, but it is neither the only method, nor the method most likely to be fruitful between the ages of seven and eleven. What is required, at least, so far as much of the curriculum is concerned, is to substitute for it methods which take as the starting point of the work of the Primary School the experience, the curiosity, and the awakening powers and interests of the children themselves' (Board of Education 1931, pp. xix–xx).

'We see that the curriculum is to be thought of in terms of activity and experience rather than knowledge to be acquired and facts to be stored. Its aim should be to develop in a child the fundamental human powers and to awaken him to the fundamental interests of civilized life so far as these powers and interests lie within the compass of childhood' (op.cit. p.75).

The Plowden Report (1967)

'A school is not merely a teaching shop, it must transmit values and attitudes. It is a community in which children learn to live first and foremost as children and not as future adults. In family life children learn to live with people of all ages. The school sets out deliberately to devise the right environment for children, to allow them to be themselves and to develop in the way and at the pace appropriate to them. It tries to equalise opportunities and to compensate for handicaps. It lays special stress on individual discovery, on first hand experience, and on opportunities for creative work. It insists that knowledge does not fall into neatly separate compartments and that work and play are not opposite but complementary' (CACE 1967, p.187).

'Some people, while conceding that children are happier under the modern regime and perhaps more versatile, question whether they are being fitted to grapple with the world which they will enter when they leave school. This view is worth examining because it is quite widely held, but we think it rests on a misconception. It isolates the long term objective, that of living in and serving society, and regards education as being at all stages recognisably and specifically a preparation for this. It fails to understand that the best preparation for being a happy and useful man or woman is to live fully as a child. Finally it assumes, quite wrongly, that the older virtues, as they are usually called, of neatness, accuracy, care and perseverance, and the sheer knowledge which is an essential of being educated, will decline. These are genuine virtues and an education which does not foster them is faulty' (op.cit. p.188).

First hand experience, activity, creative work, curriculum width, the Project or Topic approach, and quality were underlined. Do later reports still substantiate these?

'The Primary Survey' (1978)

'Children's own experiences frequently provided the basis for language work. Children were asked to talk and write about things which had happened to them out of school hours in about four-fifths of the classes. In a similar proportion of classes, school visits or school journeys provided the impetus for work in language.

'The classroom, the school and its surroundings were extensively used to provide starting points for language activities. Approximately three-quarters of the 7 year old classes and nearly three-fifths of the older groups wrote and talked about animals, plants and things which were to be seen within the school, and nearly half the classes had produced work which was based on features of the school grounds or the immediate surroundings' (DES 1978, p.50).

The School Curriculum (1981)

Emanating from the above report came 'The School Curriculum' (DES 1981). It said:

'Primary schools aim to extend children's knowledge of themselves and of the world in which they live, and through greater knowledge to develop skills and concepts, to help them relate to others, and to encourage a proper self confidence. These aims cannot be identified with separate subject areas, nor can set amounts of time be assigned to the various elements. Often a single activity promotes a variety of skills' (op.cit. p.10).

'The schools must, however, provide a wide range of experience, in order to stimulate the children's interest and imagination and fully to extend pupils of all abilities. There is no evidence that a narrow curriculum, concentrating only on the basic skills, enables children to do better in these skills' (ibid.).

'. . . children's curiosity about their physical and natural environment should be exploited; all pupils should be involved in practical as well as theoretical work in elementary science, to develop skills of observation and recording' (op.cit. p.11).

'Art and craft are included in the curricula of all primary schools; H.M. Inspectors' survey found that children would benefit if their work were based more often than it is on direct observation and study' (op.cit. p.12).

The Practical Curriculum (1981)

'Learning through experience'

'Early explorations of their environment teach children to look around them, to touch and to feel, to listen, smell and taste . . . .

'The main concern of Infant teachers is to help their pupils to explore their immediate environment and find the words to describe and discuss it effectively . . .

'The success of a Nursery or Infant school is rightly measured by how its teachers help their pupils to a wide and active experience of their world, and what their pupils learn from this experience.

'Her Majesty's Inspectors' survey of primary schools showed how important this is for older pupils too. The schools whose children did best at the basics were those which emphasized other kinds of experience too, in art, music, history, geography and science. In educational development, the privileged are those whose experience stimulates their imagination, extends their use of language, demands thought and illustrates new concepts.

'There is of course a close link between these different kinds of experience of the world and many familiar school subjects. Unfortunately teachers of older children have often tended to emphasize the content of their subjects instead of their importance as ways of experiencing and knowing the real world' (Schools Council 1981, pp.18–19).

The Cockcroft Report (1982)

'The experiences of young children do not come in separate packages with "subject labels"; as children explore the world around them, mathematical experiences present themselves alongside others. The teacher needs therefore to seek opportunities for drawing mathematical experience out of a wide range of children's activities. Very many curriculum areas give rise to mathematics. . .. Environmental education makes use of measurement of many kinds and the study of maps introduces ideas of direction, scale and ratio.

'When planning the activities of the classroom, and especially any extended topic or project work, it is therefore necessary for the teacher to try to identify at the outset the mathematical possibilities which exist within the work which is planned' (DES 1982, p.95).

Microcomputers and Mathematics in Schools (1983)

The link between good Primary school practice and the computer can be cemented when we turn to the latest report available to us:

'Most Primary classrooms are organized in ways which facilitate individual work or work in small groups. In consequence there is a noteworthy difference between Primary and Secondary schools. Where only one machine is in the classroom, in the Primary school it is more likely to be in the hands of the children, whereas in the Secondary school it is more likely to be in the hands of the teacher' (Fletcher 1983, p.5).

The question is, are we going to put the computer into the hands of the child constructively — so that it will enhance and improve, or are we going to do so destructively — so that it detracts from, and dilutes, those methods that have taken a century to nurture and develop?

Into practice — Why?

By relegating the micro computer to a 'programmed-learning' machine the proponents of this course of action are doing the micro a gross disservice. Children will soon come to associate the machine with the dull and repetitive, for the electronic magic will soon wear off; and the micro has so much more to offer.

So, in the light of our discussion on children's learning by first-hand experience let us consider the place of the computer in the Primary classroom. How will it 'fit' naturally and positively, to support and enhance good practice? How might it add a 'novel' ingredient to the curriculum. For if it does support good practice, both in terms of philosophy and in the day to day management of a classroom, and (this is of paramount importance) it is easy to use and robust, then the computer will also be acceptable to the class teacher. If computers are to succeed in the classroom the teacher must be convinced — in terms of relevance, reliability, ease of use, and cost-effectiveness.

The children do not need convincing, for the micro has already taken its place as part of the technology of their generation, and many are already prepared to use it, and accept it, without fear.

But, two caveats. If the school does not introduce the micro then we must ask two questions: (1) Who is going to gain experience of the usage, and utility, of the microcomputer? (2) Those who do use it — how are they going to use it?

In answer to the first question it is already evident that computers-in-the-home will be following a similar pattern to books-in-the-home. Without intervention, this pattern will repeat itself, with some children gaining experience in the home and others being denied it. The information-rich/information-poor dichotomy will be further widened, with much more than just the artefact at stake.

Also, even if we focus our attention upon the 'haves', the pattern of sexist discrimination is already becoming evident. Why is it the boy for whom the micro is being purchased for Christmas or birthday? Why do we read this:

> The computer, too, has added another dimension to his children's lives. Entwistle and his wife Catherine decided to buy one two years ago specifically so that their children could become familiar with its operation and its potential.
> 'The response has been varied, I must say. Charlotte is not interested; she and my wife will play a game under sufferance but that is about all. Alice is keen and will type-in a program from the magazine and then play it. My son James uses it a great deal. He will read through the programs in a magazine and then write his own, with improvements.'
> Entwistle and his son write almost all their own programs (*Sinclair User* No.19, October 1983).

The answer to the second question, 'How are computers being used?', can also be found in the above quotation. Many children play games, some type-in games from magazines, and a few write their own games. This preoccupation with games is analogous to harnessing the detergent industry to blow bubbles. It is pleasurable, short term, trivial, and a waste of resource. Of course 'games' are a way into micros — just as 'play' has such a close association with learning. But let us now turn our attention to the computer in the curriculum.

Into practice — How?

The contribution that the microcomputer can make within the Junior school curriculum falls into three areas:

1 Curriculum-centred uses
2 Curriculum innovation
3 Curriculum support

By 'Curriculum-centred', I mean that the micro can be used within the framework of a topic or project; which is in many instances at the 'core' of a Junior school classroom's methodology.

By 'Curriculum innovation' I mean that new element which the computer can introduce into the classroom — the computer itself, as an artefact, and programming.

By 'Curriculum support' I mean those programs that are designed to aid children in specific curriculum areas — to aid concept formation and development, to reinforce an already learned skill, or to support the slower learning child. Most programs currently available are of this genre.

Curriculum-centred uses

The simplest way to illustrate the support that a micro can give to a class project or topic is by citing examples.

Gibraltar Point Nature Reserve (near Skegness, Lincolnshire)

A class of fouth-year Junior children (10 years plus) visited Gibraltar Point Nature Reserve for a week's residential Field Study. Each day the children visited one of the various habitats to investigate the various plants and wild life that could be found. Within the sanctuary could be found a mere (complete with two hides), fresh water marshes, salt-water marshes, arable hinterland, woodland, sand dunes, the sea-shore and the sea.

From the visit came the usual range of classroom activities. Mapping, modelling the habitat areas; clay models of birds and creatures; observation drawings of specimens seen and brought back to the classroom (with the Warden's permission!). The setting up of fresh water and salt water aquaria. Microscope work. Soil samples. The drawing of accurate plans of the Coastguard station in which we stayed; an accurate plan view of the meandering of a river drawn from the measurements taken on-site. An account of the visit contained in a day-to-day diary that was painstakingly written up in beautiful italic hand, in black-inked fountain pen.

This formed each child's individual booklet of the topic, which is the normal format of presentation throughout the school. Anyone who has thumbed through *The Country Diary of an Edwardian Lady* (Holden 1977) will have seen a very similar record to the ones our children keep.

Any Junior school teacher entering the classroom over the next nine weeks would feel 'at home' with such a project. What they would perhaps admire would be the quality of the children's work in the various media, and the enhancement that this was given by the teachers' presentation. In other words, good Primary school practice.

However, to this very typical project was added the microcomputer.

During their stay the children had made many recordings of bird sightings. To collate these, and to allow sorting and comparisons, the information was placed within a database. A database was 'constructed' called 'Birdwatch' which enabled the children to record:

Species
Date
Time (24-hour clock)
Number (number counted/50 + /100 − 200 + /etc.)
Zone (habitat)
Behaviour
Food
Observer(s)

What is important about this database is that it was 'constructed' by the children using a *modifiable database*. By this I mean that the 'fields' did not come pre-recorded on the program. The children had to decide what 'labels' they wished to use to enter the information, and then, using the prompts of the database creator, they designed *their own* database. Programming was *not* required — just a simple response to the question on the screen.

Q. What do you wish to call the first field?
A. Species
Q. Will the data in this field be alpha, numeric or mixed?
A. Alpha (This then acts as a check for the later response to the question
        'Species?' when the database is operational)
Q. What do you wish to call the second field?
    etc.

A blank answer to the last question followed by 'Return' concludes the creator procedure, and the computer then creates the database for the children's use.

By creating their own databases the children learn how to use the micro as a tool, and also gain considerable insights into the management of data and information. In fact, in the 'Birdwatch' records the computer was unable to differentiate between male and female of the species because the children had not constructed a field for this information. Therefore a modification became necessary to insert this field into the record.

At a later stage, when children required additional information for their topic, another database was created, from the same creator program, called 'Birdsearch'. This enabled children quickly to gain access to further information on a particular bird from the resources available in school:

Species
Illustration

Detailed information
Brief information
Breeding
Eggs
Migration
Class expert

To each field was then added the 'best' book, chapter and page for that particular information.

Again, the important factors are that (a) the children constructed their own database. (Indeed, 'class expert' was added at a later date, because often it was found that there was a particularly knowledgeable child on a particular species of bird.); (b) the children sorted through the reference material themselves to determine which book was 'best' for a particular aspect. (In itself this was a positive learning experience!); (c) the computer returned the children to the source of literature to retrieve information, rather than spoon-feeding them with text. The information, and particularly the illustrations, were far superior in the book to those available on the screen so that it would have been erroneous to dilute the quality for the sake of computerizing data.

Contact with the Warden of the Reserve continued after the children had returned to school. Each week he would write a letter updating the information that the children had gathered on site. The Little Terns that the children saw arriving at Easter were now nesting. Later they lay eggs; and so forth. Here another form of database was utilized. This one was entitled a 'free-form' database, and it enabled any text to be input, and then a search called to retrieve information from that text.

In practice what happened was that, as a letter arrived from the Warden, the children would type the letter, in its entirety, into the database, and then save this data alongside all the other letters on cassette. If a child was undertaking research into, say, the Little Tern, then that child would press F for 'Find' on the menu and then type in Little Tern. Then each paragraph of each letter that has a reference to the Little Tern in it would be displayed on the screen. The child then had the option of reading the details off the screen, or printing off the details onto a small printer to take away to follow up at that child's table.

One of the factors that is hindering the development of the micro in the classroom is the very limited vision of some teachers concerning what a micro is. It is not necessarily a machine that is controlled by a typewriter!

A group of children in this project were studying the migration patterns of some of the birds that arrived at Gibraltar Point. This they were able to communicate to the computer by the use of a digital plotter. This looks, and works, rather in the manner of a pantograph, with the children placing a map of Europe, the Mediterranean and North Africa on a tablet and then tracing over the map with a small cross-wired lens attached to an arm (Figure 3.1). Single-letter entries on the keyboard then allowed the map to be coloured-in/hatched/rescaled/modified/re-orientated/annotated etc.

Having drawn in the map — literally within minutes of first being shown the digital plotter — the children then traced arrows to illustrate the flight patterns of birds leaving, or returning to, Gibraltar Point. Now, with the software *in-situ*, ask for a bird from the menu provided and its flight pattern is traced onto the map — before your very eyes!

Once more, the importance of the exercise is that the children constructed the diagram and fed in the information themselves.

Finally, another item of add-on equipment. There are on the market several keypads that can be attached to the computer. We obtained a hundred-square board called a 'Presfax' (Figure 3.2).

This tablet enables overlays to be placed on the board and either question-and-answer routines to be developed, or, by pressing any part of the overlay, information can be displayed on the screen concerning that section of the overlay.

The software was simplicity itself. 'What do you want to say?', the computer asks. The child types in the information.

'Where do you want to say it?' The child presses the illustration at those places where she wants that information to be displayed.

The applications are endless. In this instance the children drew a map to go alongside a scale model of the Nature Reserve. Look at the model, and select an area of interest. Find the area on the map. Press the map at that point, and onto the screen comes the relevant text. Here the children had chosen to store information relating to the ecology and food chains of the various habitats. The model and the map illustrated the proximity of the varied habitats — sea, littoral, saltwater, fresh water, mere, dune, arable hinterland. The micro then gave the added dimension of enabling the model to give forth detailed information about that habitat. Any additional information can be added at a later date. Simplicity itself — integrating, as it does, art, illustration, mapwork, writing skills and a practical application for the computer.

In this example the micro was embedded in a geographical/natural history slanted project. Of interest might be how the same software and peripheral equipment supported a project with a mainly historical bias.

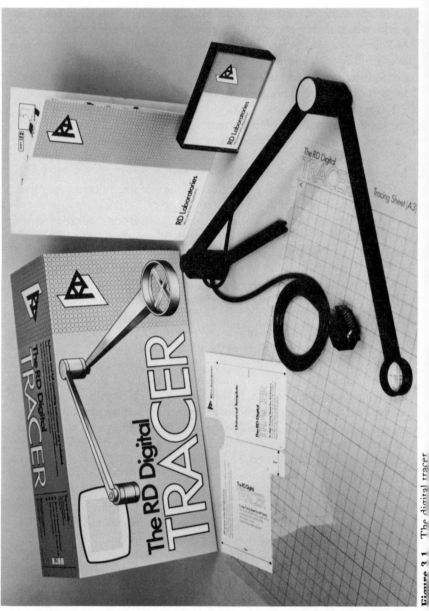

Figure 3.1   The digital tracer

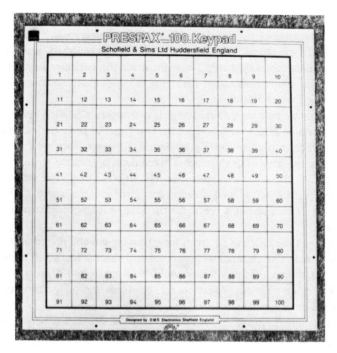

Figure 3.2 The Presfax board

Abbeydale Industrial Hamlet (Beauchief, Sheffield)

In the twelfth century the monks of Beauchief Abbey exploited the unique position of their community, through the propinquity of water-power, coal, wood and iron ore, by turning to the manufacture of agricultural implements. After Henry VIII had attacked the parent organization, the industrial settlement became 'privatized', and over the centuries became an industrial community with the manager's and workers' homes cheek-by-jowl with their place of work. It survived as a working community into this century, and has latterly been renovated into an industrial museum of the first order. If you have a class of Junior/Middle children, and are in the vicinity, do visit it — you will be amply repaid. Watch out especially for 'Working Days' when the hearths are lit, the water wheel revolves and the tilt-hammers thump. Magic indeed!

Three of our classes of 10 and 11 year olds visited the hamlet and on their return to school worked on the settlement as a place of industry and a place to live — technology and social study (although not labelled as such).

On the technological side, alongside working models made by the children of the water wheel and valve gear, tilt-hammer and camshaft, was a detailed painting undertaken by two girls to illustrate the entire process of ore-to-scythe. The whole illustration fitted the 30 cm square necessary for it to overlay the Presfax board.

Having completed the picture the girls then wrote a detailed description of each illustration of the process. Perhaps two pages or three per picture — for our children are used to writing at length. However, they were now faced with a new challenge. For the teacher asked them to trim the writing down to a total of 240 characters and spaces, or less. In other words one screen-full of text per picture — or one Ceefax page, to use the current electronic equivalent. This was not a précis for the sake of it, but précis-writing for a purpose!

Even then their task was not over, for screen lay-out and presentation had to be considered. The children were given a grid sheet (Figure 3.3) onto which to transfer the text. Thus spacing could be organized to prevent that well-known computer malady, 'wrap-round' of words cut off part-through and completed on the following line.

Thus the illustration of the room where the blades were sharpened now was supported by the text:

THE GRINDING HULL. THREE MEN WOULD SIT STRADDLE LEGGED OVER A SPINNING GRINDING WHEEL AND RUB THE BLUNT KNIFE ON THE SPINNING WHEEL. THIS IS TO SHARPEN THE BLADES.

Finally the two were matched up so that the picture of the Abbeydale process overlaid the Presfax keyboard and the relevant data were keyed in.

'Where do you want to say it?' The illustration is pressed in the relevant areas.
'Locations 29 and 30 — is this correct Y/N?'
Press Y and the job is done!
Easy!

Concurrently with this, a group of boys was making a scale model of the hamlet, allied to a map.

Show interest in a particular building, find it on the map, and press. 'This is the manager's house . . .'.

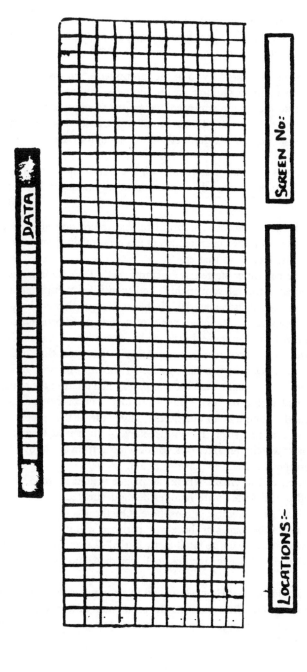

Figure 3.3   Grid squares used for text transfer

Other groups could be working on similar lines — which shows how this approach can be one solution to the vexing logistical problem of one computer and thirty-plus children. Thus:

(i) The computer fits 'naturally' into the 'group-work' classroom.
(ii) A group of two to four children can be supported by the computer at any one time. And the 'group approach' works to a strength of the computer — its ability to generate discussion of a purposeful kind, which is something that perhaps we don't encourage enough in the well-regulated classroom.
(iii) The computer in the classroom can be servicing several groups concurrently, if the work is data-composition and input, or data-retrieval and analysis.

On the social side, alongside a beautiful full-size recreation of a Victorian worker's living room, in the classroom, went a computer-aided analysis of the census data for the hamlet in that era.

Once again the computer started as an empty 'set'. The children designed the database, created the relevant 'fields', and then filled them from a close scrutiny of the original census material. Higher reading skills were brought to the fore — to decypher the Victorian hand, to decode the shorthand entries, and to cope with the calligraphic quirks of the particular enumerator.

The Inspector whose comment, when he saw the work that had been undertaken, was, 'Now that you have collected this information, next year you'll be able to use it straight from the computer', had misread the situation. We are concerned with a process — not a product. The process of learning how to harness the computer to our needs. Short cuts of the 'prepackaged' kind are irrelevant at this stage. If you disbelieve — then read Piaget!

Another project which illustrates this was developed from a visit by some of our children to the Derbyshire village of Eyam.

Eyam is famous as the village where the plague visited in 1665, and the villagers stayed put, despite entire families being decimated.

The village has an incredible atmosphere. On the doors of the Plague Cottages are written the names of those who perished within, in red! Family graves can be visited where entire families are buried — away from habitation. Within the parish church are the records of all who died, and the dates of their deaths.

Well! What would you do? How would you fit a computer into this project? If you have imagination, and appreciate the excitement of learning alongside children, then put the computer into your project. That's where it belongs — curriculum-centred.

Weather

The databases described so far have all been of a 'creator'-base format, where the children have chosen the field titles, and have constructed the database from 'scratch'. However there are occasions where perhaps a predetermined format is necessary.

One such program that we have had constructed for us is 'Weather'.

Many classes in many schools undertake a weather study at some time or other, and, as this necessitates the collection of data, and its subsequent display (in bar, pie and rose format), it seemed an eminently suitable application for the micro.

Initially the children are asked to observe the scientific instruments and then key in:

> day: month: year:
> maximum temp (C):   minimum temp (C):
> precipitation: (m/m)
> windforce: (Beaufort scale, à-la Ladybird
>   book)
> wind direction: (8 points)
> cloud cover: $(0, \frac{1}{4}, \frac{1}{2}, \frac{3}{4}, 1)$
> barometric pressure: (can be skipped)

In each of the above there are built-in fail-safe traps. For example; for the field 'maximum temperature' feed it too high a reading and the computer responds with:

> MAXIMUM TEMPERATURE RECORDED
> IS 38 DEGREES CENTIGRADE
> AT TONBRIDGE IN KENT IN 1868
>
> IF YOUR TEMPERATURE IS CORRECT THEN
> DO NOT PROCEED FURTHER, DISCUSS IT
> WITH YOUR TEACHER AND CONTACT THE
> GUINNESS BOOK OF RECORDS, OTHERWISE:
>
> PRESS 'SPACE BAR' TO CONTINUE.

At the end of the statistical-data input the screen changes to allow the weather description to be given in words rather than figures. Here we are concerned with language development, and the development of 'labelling' skills. So the children are asked to choose from a menu of words that which they consider most suitable to describe:

The temperature:	freezing, cold, warm, hot, very hot.
Precipitation:	snow, sleet, drizzle, rain.
Cloud type:	
Visibility:	
etc.	

Having completed the entry process, the children are given the opportunity to check and, if necessary, change inputted data before the record is saved to disc.

A second phase of the program is then available to the children, called 'graph'. This enables any monthly data to be retrieved and displayed — either as a statistical table or as a bar chart.

Here the power of the computer is being harnessed. For whereas in the past most weather studies never reached beyond actually drawing and shading-in the bar charts, now the information retrieval is so rapid, and the display facility so immediate, that children can move into the important phase of graph and statistical interpretation. Comparisons can be made across the month in terms of prevailing wind, rainfall, temperature change and so forth, or through the months in comparing this July with last. Can comparisons lead to forecasts? How does our local micro climate compare with the regional weather forecast?

An even more fruitful area of study can be investigated if a small interface is purchased from Griffin and George which enables external devices to be coupled to even the cheapest microcomputer. Thus the children can make a propeller, attach it to a small five-volt motor, and as the wind blows, the propeller spins the motor, which in turn becomes a dynamo. The resulting current can be fed into the micro by a home-made device. Here the children can see that the computer is perfectly capable of collecting data by itself — 'automatic data capture' in the jargon.

The important point — yet again — is that the children make the equipment themselves. It does not arrive in the classroom as 'the automated weather station'.

Our world is awash with data in one guise or another — and the various forms of database now available will allow children to capture, store and retrieve that data in forms that will help them learn more about the world in which they live. 'Learn' being the operative word. Computer-aided learning has far wider horizons than the computer as a teaching-machine.

Curriculum innovation

None of the applications discussed in the previous section required any knowledge of programming at all. All were software-driven to enable the computer to become an extension of classroom-available media. We do not demand a degree in photographic paper manufacture and film development skills before we are allowed to 'use' a camera. So with the computer — it should be a readily available tool, easy to use, to relevant situations and skills.

Perhaps this is the main difference between the computer in the Primary school, and the computer in Secondary education. In the Primary school it can be used across the curriculum in 'real' applications. In the Secondary school it either becomes a teaching machine in a specific curriculum area ('How to use a micrometer without actually touching one!'), or it becomes the property of the Computer Studies Department. ('Before you can use it you must understand it! Today's lesson is Binary Numbers.'). Snatch away the camera — how dare you enjoy taking snaps without knowing about fixatives!

However, some children will want to know how the machine works. Some children will want to write programs of their own. Some already do know how it works — for they come from computer-literate homes. What a missed opportunity if the door is slammed in their face! We talk about linking home and school, and here is a golden opportunity. Let the children bring their skill into the classroom — and harness it.

Seymour Papert, with a team of researchers at M.I.T., developed a concept-forming creature called a Turtle. Turtle can draw on the floor, and/or on screen, shapes programmed into it by a child-orientated language called LOGO. Unfortunately the little creature is horrifically expensive when considered in the light of a Primary school capitation. Consequently our school introduced BIGTRAK as a substitute Turtle.

BIGTRAK is a programmable tractor which accepts a sequence of commands programmed in and then executes them. With it the children can learn distance, turn and angles, estimation skills, sequencing and computer programming. Enough has been said, and written, about BIGTRAK (Figure 3.4) for us to curtail our discussion of its merits and applications.

Perhaps the first to realize this toy's application to real learning in the classroom was Dr Mike Thorne of Cardiff University. Reference to any article of his will amply repay the reader.

More recently, there has come onto the market a mini-turtle (what are baby turtles called?) called a Zeaker. This little desk-top Turtle provides an admirable link between the 'real', concrete BIGTRAK and the 'symbolic' Screen Turtle of LOGO.

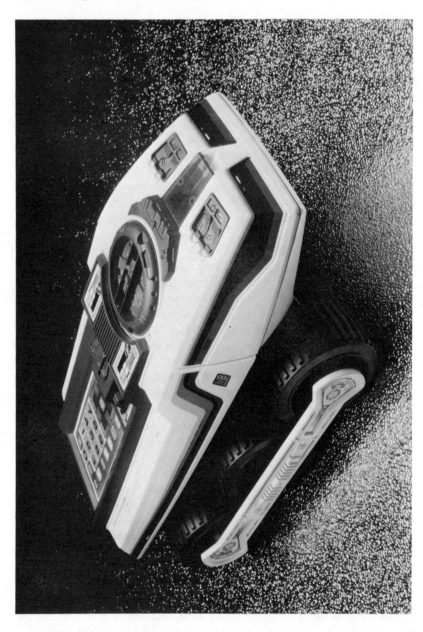

Figure 3.4 BIGTRAK

Zeaker (Figure 3.5) can be controlled from a computer by typing instructions into the micro and then executing them; and following this the program then allows children to draw directly to the computer screen — thus entering the world of computer graphics, shape and applied geometry.

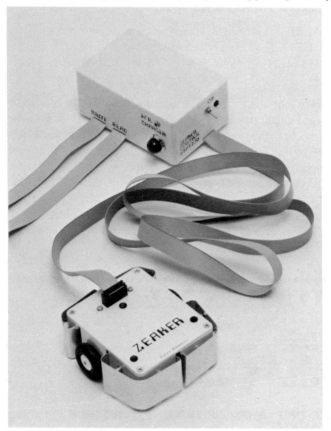

Figure 3.5 Zeaker

Once children have realized that the computer requires to be programmed in a logical step-by-step format, then they are well on the way towards writing programs of their own.

A program that provides a painless introduction into the world of computer programming is called 'DLAN'. 'DLAN' is short for Display Language, and basically all it does is to provide a series of fonts that can be used for displaying text on a screen. Additionally different borders can be called up; border, paper, and ink can be allocated different colours; and the text can be scrolled up, across or down the screen at varying speeds. Each instruction is prefaced by a line number, and the program is controlled by REM statements.

It sounds much more complicated than it is.

1. REM E1   (E = edge, and so we have set the border)
2. REM T1   (T = type, and so we have used Font 1)
3. REM = MENU(' = ' means print. This is the first printed statement on the screen).

Thus each morning a group of children descend on the cook in the school kitchens and obtain the day's menu for our multi-choice cafeteria system. A few minutes later the program is saved onto tape, and at twelve noon all the children who stay for school dinner (250 of them) can view the menu (Figure 3.6) and choose their meal for the day, before entering the dining room. As dishes become unavailable they can immediately be deleted from the display. Not only are the 'programmers' experiencing using the micro — with gratifying results — but the fruits of their labour are shared by the entire school. Daily notices of club meetings and their times are also displayed.

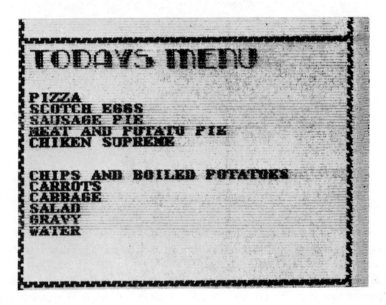

Figure 3.6 Daily menu displayed on the computer screen

Finally, some children then move on to writing programs that pass on information, or set quizzes on the various projects or topics that the class is undertaking. For example: What is the six-figure map reference of the farm house that we stayed at in Derbyshire? How many people died of the plague in Eyam in September 1665?

The more ambitious have included an introductory 'page' of a low resolution 'block-graphic' illustration, music, and a built-in scoring routine.

Interestingly, among the 'high-flyers' engaged in these activities has appeared a child who, by normal criteria, would be deemed as under-achieving. The computer has not only led to a 'success area' but its demands on rigour and accuracy, and the need to be able to read in order to follow programming books has accelerated this child's learning in the more conventional curriculum areas.

Curriculum support

This has been the growth area of Computers-in-the-Classroom now, and looks like remaining so.

As forecast by the T.E.S. in March 1982, 'predictions are that this cottage industry will largely be displaced as the major publishers finally come to dominate, a development that many educators welcome' (Taylor 1982). We are currently in the transition stage where the first fruits of their labours are beginning to reach the Primary school's door — either by mail-shot or, less likely, by cassette or disc.

Will these commercial packages be an improvement on the cottage industry prototypes? The quality should certainly be there from the programming side — but what about the educational content? This is where the centre of power lies with the teacher. For we are the paying public; we are the market: and the publishers will produce most of what we purchase most of. As teachers we need to know what we are looking for, and what we are looking at.

This is where the LEA has a responsibility, both to train teachers, and to make software available. For some LEAs the responsibility is to undo the damage that has already been done! Schools have been encouraged to purchase a micro under the DOI scheme in advance of any apparent thought as to such fundamental aspects as: Which machine, cassette or disc drive? What do we want in the way of software? Which curriculum areas do we wish to support? What training do the teachers require? Has the fundamental aspect of safety in the classroom been considered? (Young children are often being sat at mains-driven machines with many cables festooning the table top and floor — yet one machine only requires nine volts to drive it!)

Few authorities appear to have invested time and effort into research-in-depth prior to purchase, and even fewer have arrived at a philosophy and policy for introducing the micro positively into good Primary practice. Some authorities have in fact handled the situation in a most cavalier fashion by placing the mantle of computers in Primary education on the shoulders of a Secondary Adviser, or a Specialist Computer Adviser with little knowledge of the Primary classroom.

Primary education has enough of a problem living down the legacy of computers being introduced first into the Secondary schools by MEP, thus ensuring that the so-called supportive organizations of MEP and MUSE are heavily weighted towards Secondary eduction in both management and thinking.

Many in-service courses for the Primary teacher are tarred with the same brush. 'Computer programming' appears high on the agenda — yet that is the last thing that the Primary teacher needs. Have you ever seen the *length* of a good computer program? Primary teachers want to become users of the micro — confident with the hardware, and able to assess the value of the software. Courses on 'Computers in Primary Education' must have as a main ingredient 'Primary Education'! We, as Primary school teachers, cannot expect to help children become computer literate if we are not conversant with either the machine, or what it has to offer *us*.

Having attended the properly constructed courses, we should be in a position to answer the questions posed by Jeff Taylor (1982).

> 'What makes good software?'
>
> 'Is the software well-documented?'
>
> 'Be on guard for documentation that employs vague statements such as "The package is designed to assist young children in developing fundamental spelling skills" while not describing exactly what these are.'
>
> 'Does the software exploit your machine's capabilities?'
>
> 'In micros, input can be through "paddles", joysticks, light pen, etc., as well as keyboards. Output can be as graphics, animation, colour and sound, as well as text; or via an interface, through other presentation devices such as tape and video recorder, slide projectors, robots . . . .'
>
> 'Will the user be able to use the program easily and comfortably?'
>
> 'Has the software been designed with careful consideration of the intended user, or has only the machine been considered?'

'Will the program motivate the user?'

'Sound and graphics are initially captivating but do not remain so with repetition. Take note that games that interest one sex will not necessarily motivate the other and that most games designers are men.'

'Is the program easily adaptable to different users and different teaching situations?'

'Is the software appropriate for the intended teaching situation? Or because of its limitations, might it end up dictating the teaching situation?'

'Is the subject matter accurate, complete and properly sequenced?'

'Does it actually improve current practice by making learning more possible?'

'Does it allow for more learning than other media?'

'Although applicable to all categories, the criteria suggested so far pertain mostly to tutorial, and drill-and-practice programs, by far the predominant mode of CAL software. Based on the Skinnerian programmed learning model of the 60s, this variety is under serious criticism by several educationalists, who advocate more exploratory roles for the computer in education, as tool and tutee, rather than just tutor. The child programming the computer rather than "The computer programming the child", to quote Seymour Papert.[r]

'Some of these new roles are: simulations, games that are not disguised drill-and-practice, inquiry and dialogue, information retrieval, problem-solving via programming, computer aided design and word processing.'

'What learning model does the software reinforce?'

'Is the model of learning reinforced dominated by "right" and "wrong" answers?'

'Does it promote training instead of learning?'

'Does the software promote computer literacy?'

'The vast majority of CAL software actually serves to mystify the technology for pupils . . . not only psychologically damaging to the individual, this software lays an unhealthy foundation for the future person-machine relationship. . . . Is the machine portrayed as automated authority?'

'What values does the software reinforce?'

'It can be said that all software teaches something . . . countless educational games, thinly disguised drill and practice . . . simulate some aspect of warfare, revolving around endless variations of the "shoot-or-be-shot" theme . . . the teacher who uses such "motivating" material is doing little to prepare pupils for a caring society.'

I make no excuse for having quoted Jeff Taylor's article at length. We began this section with the statement that the major publishers are beginning to develop and market software aimed at the Primary classroom. The point to end on is that we are still at the birth of 'computers in the Primary school'. Will the child be benevolent or an *enfant terrible?* There is no need to be rushed into purchase. The DOI scheme might seem like a gift from on high — but it can be a costly error in terms of capitation, teacher-time, teacher-attitude and child learning if wrong choices are made.

The dangers were well highlighted by Carolyn O'Grady (1983) in an article in the *Times Educational Supplement* headlined 'Growing doubts on micros scheme'. She pointed out there that, although 11,000 schools had applied for microcomputers under the Department of Industry's scheme, there were misgivings in many authorities over the speed of this development and that some of these authorities were encouraging their schools to wait. Difficulties were being experienced over finding the additional resources to train teachers in their use and over the availability of suitable software — problems we have noted several times in earlier chapters. She quoted Michael Thorne as having said, 'In one sense the government has done the dirty on schools; they have provided the cheap bit — the hardware'. The article also indicated the concern felt in many areas over the resultant possibility of improper use of this hardware — again a problem we identified earlier.

If your authority, or your head teacher, then, asks you to purchase or use a micro in the Primary classroom, ascertain first what support you will be given. If you have already purchased or are using a micro in school, then combine with other Primary schools in your LEA and bring pressure to bear on your authority to provide the in-service support that *you* require, and to make software available for you to inspect.

Summary and conclusions

In this chapter I have sought to show that attempts to introduce the microcomputer into the Primary classroom must take the Primary classroom itself, and good Primary school practice, as the starting point, if the attempt is to be realistic, relevant, and ultimately — successful.

Having examined some ingredients of 'good practice' I then attempted to illustrate three areas where the micro can be seen in the context of classroom method: Curriculum-centred uses; Curriculum innovation; Curriculum support.

Deliberately, I commenced and concluded with caveats. In 'Malpractice' I tried to show that the initial attempts to take the micro into the classroom were erroneous — conceptually and pedagogically. In 'Curriculum support' I have tried to indicate that the direction of software development will depend upon how knowledgeable and determined the market becomes. If we are saddled with poor software then we have only ourselves to blame — individually, perhaps; collectively, as LEAs, certainly. Between the Scylla and Charybdis of a difficult birth and problematic growth lies a possible fair voyage.

Seymour Papert (1980) has said that children should program computers, and not vice versa. In the section on 'Curriculum-centred uses' I took programming to include the child's control over the micro, to use it as any other piece of classroom apparatus or media. The computer should be seen as the 'empty vessel' to be filled and used by the child, rather than the child being the *tabula rasa* to be programmed by the micro.

Tom Stonier in his book *The Wealth of Information* (1983) says 'An educated workforce learns how to exploit new technology, an ignorant one becomes its victim'.

Programs that reduce the computer to a programmed-learning machine, programs that bore or put children off, programs that crash, or are ill conceived, programs that allow teaching to stand in the way of learning will do the cause of the computer in the Primary classroom no good.

Again, Seymour Papert has said that 'There is a world of difference between what computers can do and what society will choose to do with them' (op.cit. p.5). As teachers we should re-phrase this to say, 'There is a world of difference between what computers can do and what Primary education will choose to do with them!'

Before we leave the world of the Turtle, one final thought. Seymour Papert set the 'computer and the young child' off to a magnificent start with his three-dimensional, problem-solving creature called Turtle. Why '5 × 3 = ?' and 'Cloze Procedure' followed from his inspired start only the MUSE know.

However, while the next stage in his process — that of transferring children into the computer via LOGO — might well be right for many children, for others the magic of controlling something external to the micro could well be sustained. Earlier we discussed the place of the microcomputer surrounded by models built by the children (after their visit to Abbeydale). How interesting (and relevant to control technology) it will be when the computer can be linked to their models. Then they will move, rotate, flash lights and make sounds to their command. But that will be another story . . .

CHAPTER 4

LEARNING WHY TO HYPOTHESIZE: A CASE STUDY OF DATA PROCESSING IN A PRIMARY SCHOOL CLASSROOM*

ALISTAIR ROSS

This chapter describes how a third-year junior class (9–11 year olds) used a microcomputer to help their analysis of a survey of people's attitudes towards their work. I would like to begin, however, with a few personal remarks on how the kind of work I describe is changing my views on what is possible and what is desirable in children's classroom learning.

Hypothetico-deductive investigation

My broad aims in teaching are to encourage children to conjecture about their world and their society, to test and to communicate their findings and thus to have a degree of control over their environment. Various skills are needed to accomplish these aims, but I believe that such skills are best acquired in the achievement of these aims, not as isolated exercises (Blenkin 1983). The necessary skills may change as society and technology change.

Many teachers would no doubt share such aims, but I feel that too many Primary school activities are based on simply 'close observation and response', and too few on helping children manipulate and order observations, and indeed to recognize that their observations are themselves socially constructed (Berger and Luckman 1971). Against this, many would

* This is an extended and revised version of an article which appeared in *Social Science Teacher* **12,** 3 (Summer 1983). The author would like to thank the Association for the Teaching of Social Sciences for permission to reproduce material which was published there.

argue that observations must necessarily precede analysis, and that therefore the Primary school's first task must be to enable children to gather as wide a range of experiential data as possible, and to categorize this. My experience using data processing techniques with children is leading me to the conclusion that, with the necessary tools, young children are capable of working in a hypothetico-deductive manner, and that this could fundamentally change the pattern and direction of many Primary school projects.

The hypothetico-deductive approach has been most clearly described by Popper (1959) with reference to how scientists work. It is in part a rebuttal of the method of procedure presumed to go on by many scientists; induction, in which a mass of data is collected, sifted and analysed to form patterns, and, if nothing is observed to contradict the pattern, then the truth (or at least an approximation to the truth) has been found and an eventual 'law of science' emerges.

Popper's argument is that scientists in fact make imaginative leaps in the dark, and then collect data that will justify such hypotheses or not. Hypotheses must be testable, and experiments are devised to test them: not to prove them true, but to see if they can be falsified. Falsification and verification, far from being symmetrical opposites, are not comparable: we can always falsify a hypothesis (however much it seems to have stood the test of time); we can nevery verify it. 'Scientific laws' are simply best approximations to date.

Medawar (1967a, p.133) writing on Popper's theory, convincingly asserts that scientists proceed not by 'hunting for facts, still less [by] . . . formulating "laws" ' but by 'building explanatory structures, *telling stories*, which are scrupulously tested to see if they are stories about "real life" '. This, it seems to me, is a paradigm for learning in the classroom. And the kind of conversations Medawar reports overhearing at the keyhole of the biological laboratory (as opposed to the misrepresentations of reasoning described in scientific papers) is strikingly similar to the kind of language teachers hear children using — and using better than before when discussing their microcomputer data analyses.

The art of science starts with conjectures that seek to explain, not with observations. Education also begins with children making and testing each other's explanations, not in 'close observation and response'. Not only is observation of this kind not a necessary antecedent to hypothesis, but the two are not even part of the same process. Observations that are consciously made to test an hypothesis are something quite different. To hypothesize successfully, children need not only to practise and see others hypothesizing: they need to be able to test hypotheses, to work with others in the testing, to be able to dispute. The processes of hypothesis-making and hypothesis-testing enable children to develop skills that help them better explain their world in other, non-classroom, contexts. As Medawar (1972 p.274) again puts it, 'A good scientist is discovery-prone', or in the words of Bruner (1961), 'Discovery, like surprise, favours the well-prepared mind.'

My argument here is, then, that data processing techniques with a microcomputer enable children to use their imaginations to make connections between items of information — to suggest correlations and to guess at causal relationships — *and then to test and justify them.* The problem with classroom activities hitherto has been the difficulty children have in testing hypotheses, in trying to see if they are true or not. There is little point in making falsifiable hypotheses — and only falsifiable hypotheses are proper hypotheses — if you cannot test whether your conjecture is justified or not. To test much information gathered in Primary school project work needs impossibly painstaking concentration on routine tasks of sorting data.

If children become adept at the hypothetico-deductive method, they then will also begin to understand a range of abstract concepts concerned with their focus of study, because these concepts are built up slowly as testable generalizations based on real information. Again, it is the *process* of concept formation that is ultimately of importance in the curriculum, not the actual concepts themselves — although it is useful sometimes to have a checklist of possible concepts that children might edge towards.

This analysis was not complete when I began work with my class on the case study described below. It has been worked out — is still being worked out — as I attempt different data processing techniques with children (Ross 1982, 1983a, b, 1984).

Social Studies

My class of 9 and 10 year olds were working on a study of people's perceptions and attitudes towards how work is organized. The study had originated with some of the materials in the *People Around Us* series unit called *Work*, a social studies unit for 8–11 year olds published by ILEA (1980a).

In the case study, children used a microcomputer to help analyse the results of a survey they had made of the attitudes to work and experiences of passers-by. This work was undertaken by third-year juniors, but there are evidently opportunities for similar work to be undertaken by older children. All Secondary schools have at least one microcomputer (and all Primary schools have the opportunity to purchase one). The consensus of opinion seems to be that the use of computers in schools should not be confined to computer studies departments, or even only the 'hard' sciences and mathematics, but should extend, where appropriate, to assist learning in any discipline.

There are particular arguments why Secondary school social science teachers should be closely involved in microcomputer work. Computers can be used to handle and manipulate social data in such a way that information about real or realistic individuals can be related to the more abstract and generalized groupings of the social scientist. In this way the limitations and potentialities of abstract conceptualizations can be seen more easily by the student. The machine can help the student to move rapidly between microsocial studies and numerically large-scale groups, such as those of class or gender. For example, a database of, say, 400 fictionalized individuals, with details of the occupation, sex, income and relationships of each, would provide a most useful tool in examining the problems of using the Registrar General's/OPC's definitions of social class: students could examine a few individuals in detail and then quickly relate these individuals to categorizations based on the whole set. Just as important, social science teachers could raise those ethical and social problems connected with the maintenance and use of data banks on the population which were identified in Chapter 1 as an important but often neglected dimension of computer studies. This is perhaps an unlikely topic to be raised in computer studies departments, and one for which a 'social' perspective is particularly necessary.

Social studies is the broad area of the curriculum concerned with how people organize themselves in society. It includes the study of our own social groupings, that of other cultures, and that of societies in the past. Social studies has tended to be an untidy area in Primary schools, and rather parochial (Rogers 1968). Over the past decade it has, in places, become better intellectually organized and more rigorously defined, in particular through the work of Denis Lawton (1971) and of Alan Blyth and the History, Geography and Social Studies 8–13 Schools Council project team (1976). In Primary schools, social studies can be described as having three elements:

— a concern with the processes of understanding and evaluating evidence, and of recognizing the tentative nature of conclusions;

— a willingness to use children's own social experiences (of family, friendship groups and school, for example) both as valid evidence and as a starting point for wider enquiry; and

— an overriding concern that children develop social concepts that will enable them to understand and compare the underlying social structure of groups and societies.

ILEA's curriculum guidelines in social studies (1980b) sought to help children establish for themselves concepts of the division of labour, power and authority, tradition, social control, social change, conflict, cooperation and interdependence. *People Around Us* was designed to this end.

The class had discussed the different ways in which various jobs might be categorized (in terms of income, or of length of training, or of how much they would be missed). They had examined the organizational hierarchies of their own and local schools and (through a book) of a factory. They had talked at length about sex roles and working. I now wanted them to juxtapose this work with some wider perceptions of work to be obtained by devising, conducting and analysing a social survey of passers-by. I hoped that this would provide them with evidence that would make them re-evaluate their earlier hypotheses; that they would be introduced to some of the problems and skills of sampling; and that they would be aware of the limitations of their survey. I also expected this to develop other educational skills and concepts, in the fields of language, mathematics and social interaction.

Hardware and software

We had been selected as one of eleven ILEA Primary schools to try to find ways in which microcomputers might assist learning in an area of the curriculum. The school was given a Research Machines Limited 380Z microcomputer, a fairly powerful machine with two disc drives and a printer. A disc drive enables additional information, stored on a small magnetized floppy disc, to be considered: the microcomputer can rapidly read the disc, transferring what is necessary to its own memory for as long as it is needed. ILEA has also provided a software package called micro LEEP, a data processing collection of programs. The class had already used this in looking at the local returns for the 1871 census in some history work (Ross 1982, 1983a).

Data processing provides the means of analysing a collection of data (or a 'file') for specified similar characteristics. It may be thought of as analogous to the use of a table of social statistics. For example, the imaginary data described above of Registrar General classifications of 400 individuals could be presented as a long table. A simple problem would be to identify each individual earning over a certain amount: obviously this could be done fairly easily by hand, running a finger down the 'income' column and reading the names on those lines which fulfil the condition. A more complex problem might be to locate all males of less than a certain age in a particular socio-economic class earning more than a certain amount, and to list them in date-of-birth order. This is the kind of task that micro LEEP could perform in two or three minutes.

There are three stages to this. One must first design the table: How many columns will there be? What will each be called? How much information will be entered for each line in the column — how big will the column need to be? In data handling terminology, each column is a field. Secondly, one must enter the information in the table; each record much have the data entered for each field. In micro LEEP, the records are keyed into the computer and stored on a floppy disc. Thirdly, one can make any number of enquiries. To do this, those characteristics which must be fulfilled for particular fields must be specified. The appropriate records will then be selected, and it is possible to specify those fields for which one requires details to be output (all fields are not usually necessary), and if these records should be sorted into any particular order.

The survey

To return to the class survey. We discussed at great length the kind of questions we might ask passers-by about their work. If we only asked open-ended questions, how much could we write down as they spoke? On the other hand, if questions only called for yes/no answers (or even a range of options), how much would we be curtailing the interviewees' answers? What questions could we properly ask of people and expect them to answer? Asking how much people earned, the class decided, was definitely out. What about age? Finally they decided that interviewers would have to estimate the age of the person being interviewed (they were able to do this with an apparently fair degree of accuracy, ie. as well as I was able to estimate!). The eventual list of questions agreed upon is shown in Figure 4.1: mostly closed questions, with some scope for open-ended replies. The questionnaires were duplicated and distributed. Armed with clipboards, we descended on Notting Hill Gate one

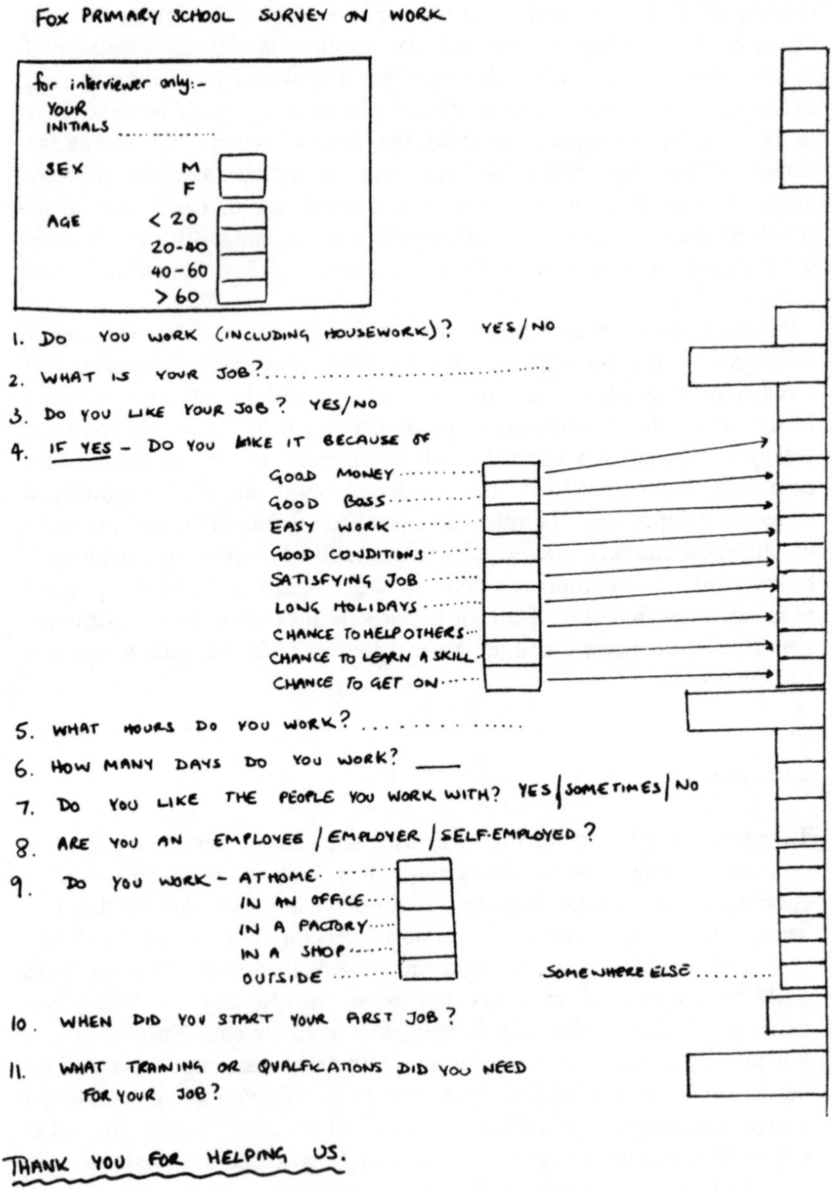

FOX PRIMARY SCHOOL SURVEY ON WORK

for interviewer only:-
YOUR
INITIALS ....

SEX   M
             F

AGE   < 20
             20-40
             40-60
             > 60

1. DO YOU WORK (INCLUDING HOUSEWORK)? YES/NO

2. WHAT IS YOUR JOB?...................................

3. DO YOU LIKE YOUR JOB? YES/NO

4. IF YES - DO YOU LIKE IT BECAUSE OF

   GOOD MONEY ....
   GOOD BOSS ....
   EASY WORK ....
   GOOD CONDITIONS ......
   SATISFYING JOB ....
   LONG HOLIDAYS ....
   CHANCE TO HELP OTHERS ...
   CHANCE TO LEARN A SKILL ..
   CHANCE TO GET ON .....

5. WHAT HOURS DO YOU WORK? . . . .

6. HOW MANY DAYS DO YOU WORK? ____

7. DO YOU LIKE THE PEOPLE YOU WORK WITH? YES/SOMETIMES/NO

8. ARE YOU AN EMPLOYEE/EMPLOYER/SELF-EMPLOYED?

9. DO YOU WORK - AT HOME ......
                 IN AN OFFICE ....
                 IN A FACTORY ....
                 IN A SHOP ......
                 OUTSIDE ......   SOMEWHERE ELSE ....

10. WHEN DID YOU START YOUR FIRST JOB?

11. WHAT TRAINING OR QUALIFICATIONS DID YOU NEED
    FOR YOUR JOB?

THANK YOU FOR HELPING US.

Figure 4.1 The final questionnaire

morning. Pairs of children working together approached any adult not obviously in too much of a hurry, and invited them to answer a few questions. The refusal rate (which we did not think to record accurately) was about 25 per cent.

In less than an hour we had completed 120 forms.

Back in the classroom we looked briefly at some simple statistics of our returns — how many males and females, how many employed, and so on. We soon discovered an error in our form: we had not thought about students, and some groups had recorded students as not working (and thus not proceeded beyond question 2), while others had taken students to be workers. It was decided that students could be considered workers, and that we should collect more survey results. We changed locale for the second series of interviews, and went to Kensington High Street a couple of days later. Here we completed 153 more returns, with a somewhat higher refusal rate (33 per cent). This change in location made it necessary to add the information to the survey forms (N for Notting Hill Gate, K for Kensington High Street).

Again in the classroom we looked at our findings and discussed some of the more elaborate questions about people's attitudes that we might be able to ask when a data file had been constructed. Why did people like their job? Who had we actually interviewed, by age and by sex? Who liked their work best? What sort of jobs were there? How had people trained for their work? Were there differences between those interviewed in Kensington High Street and those in Notting Hill Gate? Before such questions could be answered, the data file had to be compiled and consulted.

Coding

Several children in the class then devised a file structure for the data (deciding on the nature of the fields), while everyone was engaged upon coding and entering the data for the records. Simple coding was a useful way of shortening data: it is quicker to type M then MALE, and there are fewer chances of error. Seventeen fields were created:

Field	Length	Notes
LOC(ation)	1	K(ensington) or N(otting Hill)
INT(erviewers)	4	Initials of pair of children conducting the interview
SEX	1	M(ale) or F(emale)
AGE	2	Estimated age range

WORKER	1	Y(es) or N(o), worker or not
JOB	18	Description of job, in words
LIKE JOB	1	Y or N, do you like your job
BECAUSE	9	Numbers 1 to 9, or any combination; a number for each reason
HOURS	2	Average number of hours worked a day
DAYS	1	Average number of days worked a week
PEOPLE	1	Y or N do you like the people you work with
POSITION	2	(Employ)EE, (Employ)ER, or S(elf)-E(mployed)
WORK LOC(ation)	11	Where do you work, in words
FIRST JOB	4	Date when work started
QUALI(fication)	15	Qualifications for job, in words
JOB CODE	3	Coding of job
Q(ualification) CODE	3	Coding of qualification

The last two fields were particularly interesting. Two groups of children devised a complicated coding system for all the jobs and qualifications found. The class had already used a coding system of nineteenth century occupations in their work on the 1871 census. That coding was taken from *Nineteenth Century Society* (Armstrong and Booth 1972) and the class had appreciated the advantages in analysis of using a numeric code that linked similar kinds of work; all those involved in trading, for example, had a code commencing in 5, subsequent digits creating sections and subsections within the category. However, this nineteenth century code was unsuitable for our survey results; there were no entries for the television producer, the word processor or the football coach the class had interviewed. A new code was drawn up in which the first digit, as in Armstrong, indicated the broad category of occupation (manufacturing, domestic, trading, etc.) The second digit indicated a more precise job within the broad category, and the final digit the position of the interviewee within the organizational hierarchy (all managers' codes ended with 2, all apprentices' codes with 7 and so on). It was not always possible to assign this last digit with any accuracy. A similar code was devised for the qualifications that interviewees had said were necessary for their job.

The devising of these codes, their application and use, were educationally very important. It seems highly desirable that children (and adults) should realize that categories and generalizations like this are merely heuristic devices, often helpful in analysis (but sometimes misleading); that they are devised and used by people (who often make mistakes in classification); and that there can be real dilemmas over how to apply a classification in marginal cases. Two code books were produced for each code, one in alphabetical order and the other in numerical, or code order.

The coding was done on the questionnaire itself, in the boxes down the right-hand margin (extra boxes being needed for the fields LOC, JOBCODE and Q CODE). The data was then keyed into the microcomputer by groups of two or three children at a time. Small groups like this worked well and accurately: one child read out the information, one typed and the third checked the display on the monitor for accuracy. Although it took a week to enter all 272 records, this only amounted to $1-1\frac{1}{2}$ hours work per child, and had the great advantage of impressing upon the class that they themselves were the source of the computer's information.

Analysis

While this was going on, we were also discussing, formally and informally, the kinds of problem and question that we might use the microcomputer to help solve. For example, did we interview a fair selection (or sample) of the population? Did people in Notting Hill have different kinds of work from those in Kensington? Did they find different kinds of satisfaction in their work? Did men like their jobs more than women? What was the range and distribution of occupations found? Who was unemployed?

The process of interrogation is by typing in specifications in response to a prompt on the monitor screen. Questions are phrased in Boolean logic, specifying conditions that must be matched in a particular field. For example, SEX = M specifies a field (SEX), a conditional relationship (=) and a condition to be fulfilled (that the field must contain M). A more elaborate enquiry might isolate a particular group of workers using that JOBCODE field: the printout shown in Figure 4.2 is a response to an enquiry to list all people whose work was involved with education (having JOBCODES between 711 and 739). The nonsense of the inductive approach is displayed at this point. The total number of enquiries (or hypotheses) possible with this database is about 36 million million million. The inductive approach would suggest that we simply wallow around in this until correlations appear. What the children did — and what any working social scientist, historian or whatever would do — was to make explanations and to test and see if they fitted the data. If they were falsified, they were abandoned: if not, they were further tested and used to erect more elaborate explanations.

```
Micro LEEP    Enquiry

Filename.........WORK82
Your Enquiry......JOBCODE>710 AND
                  JOBCODE<740

OUTPUT to.........Screen Printer
Print Format......3
Fields for Output..JOB QUALI AGE SEX
                   FIRSTJOB WORKLOC
                   LIKEJOB PEOPLE

JOB              QUALI            AGE SEX FIRSTJOB WORKLOC      LIKEJOB PEOPLE

PROFESSOR        GRADUATE COURSE  50  M   1969     UNIVERSITY   Y       Y
LECTURER         DEGREE           30  M   1969     LABORATORY   Y       Y
LECTURER         DEGREE           30  M   1967     UNIVERSITY   Y       Y
TEACHER          DEGREE           30  M   1966     SCHOOL       Y       Y
TEACHER          DEGREE           30  M   1966     SCHOOL       Y       Y
LECTURER         DEGREE           30  M   1963     OFFICE       Y       Y
LAWYER           STUDYING         30  F   1965     HOME OFFICE  Y       Y
TEACHER HOUSEWIFE COLLEGE         30  F   1963     HOME SCHOOL  Y       Y
TEACHER          DEGREE           30  M   1978     SCHOOL       Y       Y

The file is  272  records long

 9  Records matched

END OF Micro LEEP
```

Figure 4.2 Printout showing result of enquiry to list all people with jobs connected with education.

Particular explanations were assigned to groups of two or three children. Each group was asked to try to find ways of analysing the data and producing some kind of display to demonstrate their findings and justify their hypotheses. This was, if possible, to be both in some graphical form (bar chart, pie chart etc.) and through some written conclusions. A great deal of intra-group discussion followed, about what they were being asked to discover, about how to describe effectively and delimit the groups they were interested in when formulating their microcomputer enquiry, and about interpreting their computer printout. As each group concluded their work, they took on a fresh problem, usually one arising out of the conclusions they had reached in the earlier problem. Occasionally groups worked together towards a conclusion, but more often they simply tended to utilize other groups' findings in the interpretation of their own work. I had intended to try to monitor carefully all the enquiries in progress, but I eventually lost track of some of what was going on. Over the three weeks' duration of the project, probably some 70 enquiries were made, some of which involved three or four micro searches.

A relatively simple example: one group decided to find out what they could about the interviewees who said they had no job. Their initial microcomputer enquiry was simply to ask for all records where WORKER = N. The only fields that could be output for this (see the questionnaire) were SEX and AGE. In order not to get a long and jumbled list, the sexes were separated in the printout, the group specifying SEX as the field to be sorted: all females (F) were listed before males (M). The printout was used to analyse the information: children used different coloured pens to mark and sort groups by age, and were thus able to add up the totals for each age group, males compared with females. However, they decided that having found that, for the age group 20–40, there were 11 unemployed females and 22 unemployed males, was not enough. A parallel enquiry had to be made of all those in employment in order to make an effective comparison. It was also necessary to compare these findings with the conclusions of the group looking at the overall ratio of males to females interviewed.

This group, looking at the ratio of the sexes interviewed, produced most interesting conclusions. A very simple enquiry produced the fact that they had interviewed 158 males and 114 females, a 58:42 ratio. There was much discussion on both the significance of, and reasons for this. I asked 'What would you have expected to find, if it had been a fair survey?'

Andrew 'I'd expect to find about half and half.'
Me 'Why?'

Andrew 'I'd expect the boys to go and interview the men, and the girls the women, and because there are half boys and half girls in our class.'
Walter 'Most of the boys in the class might not interview just men, but if altogether there were (say) 20 people, they'd get, say, 13 men and seven women.'
Me 'More men than women. Why?'
Walter 'Well, I just think that's the way they'd be.'
Me 'What's the proportion of men and women in the country as a whole?'
Desmond 'About 51:49?'
Andrew 'But we interviewed more males.'

Andrew went on to write: 'There are two possible reasons why we interviewed more males than females. The first is that more women might stay at home to do housework and cook the dinner. But that is only one reason. The other is more complicated. It is that more people wanted to interview men. This is because they're biased. We used the computer to find out which groups (of interviewers) were biased.'

They drew a pie chart for each interviewing group, showing for each the male:female ratio. Of the 14 groups, five showed a bias, one way or the other, greater than 60 per cent. Four were biased towards males (63, 75, 82 and 87 per cent) and only one towards females (62 per cent). Andrew concluded:

'We then asked people why they were biased and got some quite interesting results.'
'Trevor: He thought males might have more interesting jobs, and women looked a bit more grumpy. He thought he was biased.'
'Andrew and Walter: Thought that men looked (as if they had) more interesting jobs, and women looked a bit more grumpy. They thought they were biased.
'Katherine: Thought there were more men on the streets. She didn't think she was biased.'
'Alice: Not sure.'
'Patsy (female biased group): Thought most men had already been interviewed, and a lot of men didn't understand her when she tried to interview them. She didn't think she was biased.'
'Anthony: Went for people who looked young. Charles (his partner) said that he went for interesting people, but Anthony disagreed with this.'

Charles also drew a cartoon of the interviewing, suggesting that there might be other reasons for bias in the sampling process.
Why did many children think that the women might have less interesting jobs? One group investigated the range of jobs that were given: men gave 89 different occupations, and women only 45. Another group looked at those who said that they disliked their work.

Figure 4.3 Charles' cartoon

'We found out', they wrote, 'that 4 per cent of the working men disliked their job and 96 per cent liked their job. Then we found out 11 per cent of the working women disliked their job, and only 89 per cent liked their job. We think that the reason is that men have more different jobs than women have, and the women who dislike their job would be perfectly happy with some of the men's jobs.'

The group then decided to tackle the problem in a different way. They looked at the reasons people gave for liking their work. They divided the interviewees according to sex, and then found out how many people gave each of the nine listed reasons. Rank-order histograms of reasons given were produced for each sex. Although they showed that the most popular reason for liking jobs was 'a satisfying job' for both sexes, there were important differences. The second reason for men was 'good money' (fourth for women), their fourth reason was 'a chance to help others' (sixth for women), and their fifth reason was 'a chance to get on' (seventh for women). On the other hand, women rated 'working for a good boss' third (men, seventh). One member of the group expressed the results in tabular form:

Reasons	Males	Females
	%	%
Good money	17	11
Good boss	6	12
Easy work	5	$3\frac{1}{2}$
Good conditions	14	14
Satisfying job	24	23
Long holidays	6	7
Chance to help others	11	10
Chance to learn a skill	7	10
Chance to get on	10	9

Another pair discovered an apparent correlation between the liking of one's job and age. Nine per cent of those under 20 disliked their work, compared with 6 per cent in the 20–40 and 40–60 age ranges, and none of the over-60s. They tried out several ways of presenting this information graphically. Firstly they used histograms, a vertical column for each age, with two different colours to show liking/disliking. This, they felt, did not show the trend very well, because of an over-representation in the sample of the 20–40 age range. They then tried four separate bar charts of age groups, with different scales, with a column for likes and a column for dislikes. This was a bit better, but they finally settled for a simple and striking graph of age against the percentage disliking their work.

The examples above show how part of the work of many groups interlocked, each using information and ideas from the others. The number and quality of the discussions that occurred in this was extraordinary. There was an evident exercising of critical awareness and abilities by the children. They were suspicious of their data: of the bias in the sample, of the bias in their sampling techniques, of the possibility that they were not always being given accurate information, and of the difficulties of creating categories for analysis. Their hypotheses were tested against each other, scathingly criticized, reformulated and reappraised. The microcomputer helped in all this; it became an easily consulted and speedy reference tool, not a sci-fi gadget. But it appeared to me that the pupils were aware of its limitations, and that this was, at least in part, because it was their own information that they had loaded onto the disc. They knew the circumstances of the origin of the data (and hence its limitations), and they could also see that the computer was not producing anything more than what they had already told it. The speed, the accuracy, the convenience, the capacity: these were all factors to be marvelled at — but not the information itself.

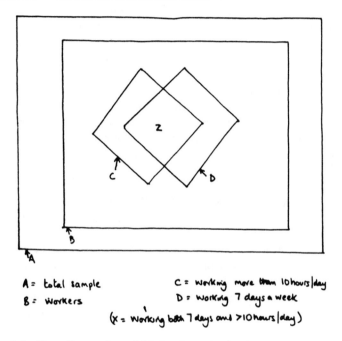

A = total sample
B = workers

C = working more than 10 hours/day
D = working 7 days a week

(x = working both 7 days and >10 hours/day)

Figure 4.4   Venn diagram by a child showing sub-sets of those working long hours.

Not all the groups worked in such an interlinked fashion. Some followed a single line of investigation through several enquiries in relative isolation. One such pair of children began by examining the reported lengths of people's working days. A histogram showed that only 25 per cent worked a 'standard' eight-hour day, while 6 per cent claimed to work 24 hours a day. They then looked at the number of days worked each week: 40 per cent worked five days a week, and 5 per cent seven days a week. 'It is amazing sometimes people work 24 hours a day without any sleep,' one child wrote. A Venn diagram was drawn to scale, to show the sets of who worked the long hours and many days: Figure 4.4 is based on their findings. They were even more surprised to find from this that 14 people worked both long hours and seven days a week. Yet another quick computer run showed that nearly all of these were housewives; but this information sent them into a further investigation — what other sorts of job involved long hours of work? Using the initial digit of the job code, the various occupations could be conveniently grouped into ten categories such as 'public service worker', 'manufacturing' and so on. A search was made for the job categories of all those who worked over ten hours a day or for seven days a week. The largest groups, about 30 per cent, were in the 'domestic work' category (mostly housewives), followed by 9 per cent in 'entertainment'. No other category had more than four workers in it. This in itself was not very revealing, they felt. It was necessary to compare this ranking with the distribution of workers who had relatively short hours — less than ten hours a day or less than seven days a week. The rank order was very different here: 'manufacturing' and 'trading' workers dominating (18 per cent each), with 'domestic work' trailing at seventh place (7 per cent) and 'entertainment' at ninth place (2 per cent).

One group analysed the categories of jobs in the working population of our sample (using the first digit of the JOBCODE). Their distribution charts and graphs showed a range from 15 per cent of the sample working in each of the two categories manufacturing and retailing, to 2 per cent in agriculture. ('That's not surprising, you wouldn't find many of them round here,' said one in discussion later.) Jobs in education and the professions were also strongly represented (32 people, 14 per cent). I asked why there were relatively so many people involved in the three largest categories: 'Because we asked the questions in London, and those are the kind of jobs people are likely to do in London.'

Work places were also investigated. 'More people work in offices than anywhere else,' they reported. 'Older people tended to work in offices, and more younger people in shops. We think that this is because the people who work in offices need more skills than the people who work in shops' (i.e. older people would have more skills). They drew a complex bar chart to show this relationship. Meanwhile a parallel group had been testing not the relationship of age to workplace, but of interview location to workplace. They found marked differences between the two places. Although office-based workers were the largest group in each location, the proportions were different — 40 per cent of workers in Kensington High Street, compared with 28 per cent in Notting Hill Gate. 'We found more office workers in Kensington High Street because offices need more facilities,' they concluded. On the other hand, there were twice as many shop workers in Notting Hill Gate (15 per cent) than

Kensington High Street (7 per cent). 'We were rather surprised . . . because on Kensington High Street they have bigger shops so they need more people to work there. But it is possible that at the certain time we interviewed people in Kensington most of them were working.'

Some enquiries came to a dead end: one group, for example, found that the information contained in the field POSITION was not very useful. They thought that this was because many of the people who had been interviewed had given contradictory answers to this question. Another group found that we had a very skewed sample as far as age was concerned, with 65 per cent of our interviewees between 20 and 40 years old. Was this because old people were less in evidence on the streets at the time of the survey? Several children suggested this. Others thought that many older people might already be at work, or that older people were avoiding the rush on the streets, or that members of the class had chosen to interview younger rather than older passers-by.

A final example of the sorts of conclusion that were being reached is shown in the work on unemployment. Why were so many more men than women unemployed? One report concluded:

'Males aged 20–40 are more unemployed than females of the same age by twice as much. We thought that more females would say that they were employed, because housework is counted as being a job. But lots of men don't do housework and are unemployed as well, so they have no job. I don't think it is important that more men than women are out of work, because it would be the same if it was the other way round. But I do think it's important that people have jobs and I hope there will be no unemployed people soon.'

The ability to detect, analyse and describe women as a flexible pool of labour, and the awareness of hidden unemployment, are demonstrated with even greater clarity in the comment in discussion. 'If the women go for jobs and don't get them, then they go back to doing housework and don't call themselves unemployed.'

The work described here is a small fraction of all that happened in the classroom. The microcomputer might at first have been a motivating factor, though I think that for most children in the class this stage had passed before this particular project began. What was novel was the ability to use the results of their own social survey quickly to check out ideas, hunches, hypotheses. It could all have been done manually, from slips of paper, but this is back-breaking (or rather mind-numbing) work; the effort is not commensurate with the evaluations and discussions that follow. Also, the accuracy of hand-compiled work is always a little doubtful, and who wants to challenge someone's conclusion if it means going back to sorting our 272 forms in a different way?

I asked the class at the end of the project if they could have done the work without the computer.

'Without the computer, it would have involved seaching through piles of papers and stuff.'

'But could you have done that?'

'No.'

'We could have done it — it would have taken a lot more time . . .'

'Every single question instead of taking a couple of minutes would have taken a couple of hours.'

'Couple of *days*!'

The use of the flexible data processing package and the microcomputer enabled us to leap to and fro between the immediacy of the individual interview and the discussion about the sample as a whole: and it is in this debate that real social studies education occurs.

Summary and conclusions

People learn best if their learning task has a purpose. This belief lies at the root of the argument for a process approach to the Primary curriculum; children learn to write well if they need to write for a purpose — and moreover, for a purpose that they perceive as real. Similarly, while we could devise exercises that encourage children to make hypotheses, these are unreal, and are seen as unreal — unless it is possible to test the hypotheses properly. Hypotheses framed without the possibility of falsification, purely as the response to an exercise, are likely to be both wild and woolly. There is no purpose in making falsifiable hypotheses unless there is some possibility of checking them: Why spend time and energy making conjectures if you will never know if they are false or not?

Hypothesis-making without testing becomes wild and unrestrained guessing: when it is possible to test, *then* hypotheses become real.

In another data processing project (Ross 1982) the same group of children was looking at the census records for Kensington in 1871. Some children thought that there was a connection between age and birthplace — it seemed to them that younger people had been born locally, older people at a distance.

To make the hypothesis testable, careful thought was needed to frame it: what do we mean exactly by 'old'? Over 50? Over 40? Why? Where exactly is 'local'? From the questioning an hypothesis emerged, and was tested — and was compared to a rival hypothesis with different definitions of 'old' and 'local'.

The microcomputer doesn't possess arcane knowledge or act with mysterious powers, as far as these children are concerned. It is a tool, performing a task that they can see only too well is mind-bogglingly boring. But it can do the job quickly and accurately, and therefore it is useful. The time is thus made available for the rigours of discussion, for testing and probing each other's meanings, for deducing conclusions — for erecting structures that try to explain the world, and trying to knock them down.

Technical footnote

Micro LEEP has been replaced in ILEA by micro SCAN. Other data processing packages include QUERY (from AUCBE) and INFILE (Leicester Education Authority). The author is presently preparing with Malcolm Hall a database package for Primary and Middle schools with graphic display outputs (barcharts, maps, graphs, etc.) for Addison Wesley Ltd called DATAPROBE, which should be available early in 1985.

CHAPTER 5

WHY LOGO?

BERYL MAXWELL

It is now almost three years since I became involved with computers. Initially it was through my own teenage children studying 'Computer Studies' for an 'O' Level. As an interested mum and a teacher of young children, I was prying into the curricular changes of our Secondary schools!

Our teenagers at home began to initiate me into the mysteries of talking to a computer. It seemed that you could only communicate by talking to it in one of the languages specially designed for this purpose, and the one they were learning was BASIC. They tried to explain how it worked, but to me it was gobbledegook! This unnerved me. I began to think about how this was going to affect me as a Primary teacher.

About this time, two of our fourth-year boys at the school where I work produced a home computer. They had made a program, which they showed me, by following the instructions 'in the book'. On close questioning it was obvious that they had no idea why or how it worked. It seemed they had blindly followed the rules, and as luck would have it, the rules worked!

At once alarm bells sounded! I have spent the last twelve years in a rather different position from most of my Primary colleagues. I have worked almost exclusively in the Primary mathematics field. As a part-time teacher, I have worked daily, each school morning, with groups of children from the whole age and ability range of a two-form entry Junior school in Hertfordshire. In this role, I suspect I have spent a great deal more time than most generalist teachers in the Primary sector could ever hope to, in thinking and learning about how young children learn mathematics. Perhaps I should declare my prejudices. I am an 'A' Level Mathematics failure, but I have always had an interest in, and derived much pleasure from, teaching the subject. I know myself to be a victim of 'traditional' rote teaching, discouraged from questioning and finding my own solutions. My own failure, I am convinced, was due to my lack of understanding, so that when the rote learning failed I had nothing but tricks to rely on, and no firm foundations on which to build.

Throughout my teaching, I have tried to give children opportunities to have plenty of mathematical activity. This has often been of an investigational nature and involving practical activity. Most children need to experience, that is to do and see things, before they can begin to understand. Telling or showing is not enough for them to learn. It is through these activities, and talking about them, that they can begin to experience the patterns and relationships that are the cornerstones of mathematical thinking. By ordering their thoughts in trying to explain what is happening, they come to a better understanding. I feel too often there is a great rush to 'recording', and to 'doing sums', so that parents and headteachers may have evidence that children are being 'taught' rather than allowing them to learn.

Mathematics is a language to be communicated. Children should have the opportunity to use it as a spoken one. Too soon they are pushed from their three-dimensional world onto two-dimensional paper! We allow most children three to four years to develop their spoken language before we teach them how to read and write it. Perhaps mathematical communication should have a chance. Ask any teacher of young children what children find difficult when doing mathematics and they will often tell you it is the language that baffles them not the mathematics itself, once they understand what is required.

Why did BASIC unnerve me? Not long after my initial encounters I had the chance to attend an in-service course on Microtechnology in the Primary School. At the time most computer work was being done in the Secondary sector and within two or three Colleges of Education. A few programs for use with younger children were being written and trialed. These were very much in the drill-and-practice, structured-reinforcement vein. I wondered why these expensive machines were being employed in rote learning. Surely this powerful tool could do something else? To be used in this way did not fit in with my thinking about children having plenty of first-hand experiences. There were other programs around using the graphics facilities of the computer. For example I found myself following complicated lists of instructions on the screen, telling me to press this key and that to get coins to move into sets. I began wondering if children wouldn't learn more from actually handling coins and counting out change in a shopping situation.

Then I also met teachers, often themselves very enthusiastic about writing programs for children, very keen to teach Juniors to program in BASIC and I felt I was going to be drawn into a situation seen too often, of pushing down ideas from the higher levels of education, when I think we should be starting from the child and building up. I felt there were arguments that could be advanced for using computers in some of the ways I was seeing. What were these? It teaches logical thinking. Does teaching children BASIC do this? The computer promotes great motivation and it does away with the 'cross teacher' syndrome because it is patient. Children can acquire keyboard skills (whatever that entails!) and many other reasons are put forward to support their use with young children. However, I was still not convinced that it was worth the bother of learning how to use a computer, especially if there was only going to be one machine to share between the nine teachers and 240 children in our school! Teaching older Junior children to program in BASIC seemed a non-starter. My own teenagers seemed to spend ever-increasing amounts of time at the keyboard trying to get their programs to work. If they were anything to go by, an individual would need a great deal of time to type in his/her lists of instructions and to get it to work. It also seemed from my talks with those Junior children with 'home computers' that only the most able, at the top end of the age range, would be able to cope with using BASIC to write programs. It would certainly not give *all* the children a chance to use the machine. So what about the other programs I had seen? Unfortunately the 'testing' type of program seemed to indicate much individual working by the children at the machine. Much of my teaching has involved group activity enabling exchange of ideas, and cooperation with others in learning, and once more I felt such individual use of the machine would leave little time for much else.

I was beginning to think I had wasted four valuable days attending the course. Suddenly everything changed. I met a 'Floor Turtle'.

Introducing the 'Floor Turtle'

'What is a 'Floor Turtle'?' you may well ask. It is a dome-shaped robot on wheels. You control the robot, which is attached by a wire to the computer, by typing in a series of instructions. These make it move around the floor. It responds to simple commands, which are the first words you use of a computer language called LOGO.

LOGO was created by Seymour Papert and his colleagues at M.I.T. for use in education. (Anyone who is interested in LOGO and the philosophy behind it should read Seymour Papert's book, *Mindstorms: Children, Computers and Powerful Ideas* (1980).) LOGO begins with a Floor Turtle, which gives children a three-dimensional concrete object to think with. Having been allowed to play with a Floor Turtle on my in-service course, I became very excited about its possibilities. At the end of the course it was felt a Primary teacher should use the Floor Turtle with children, and see what would happen. I volunteered, and took the Floor Turtle into my classroom for seven days on May 11th, 18th and 19th, and from June 1st to 4th inclusively, in 1981.

This was the first time we had had a computer in school, so we spent our first lesson arranged around the computer, and the Floor Turtle, learning how to make the robot work. The Floor Turtle is motorized and carries a pen, which can be lifted up and down onto paper on the floor. You type in certain instructions on the keyboard of the computer, to enable the robot to draw pictures according to your commands. The same pictures are drawn on the screen of a monitor by a 'Screen Turtle'.

There are six simple instructions that enable you to begin. Type in,

PEN OFF (This lifts the pen, so it doesn't draw)

or

PEN ON (This puts the pen down, so it will draw)

or

FORWARD (This moves the 'Turtle' forward in its current direction, a number that you specify)

or

BACKWARD (Opposite to FORWARD!)

or

RIGHT (Moves the Turtle the number of degrees you specify turning to the RIGHT)

or

LEFT (Opposite to RIGHT)

By the time the second session had finished each child had had a chance to type in an instruction and see the Floor Turtle draw. They were then able to make shapes and drawings of their own choosing. In no time at all the children were ready to use the Floor Turtle. I had thought the equipment would lend itself well to being used by small groups of between two and four children at a time. 'Turtle Groups' were formed and they had turns 'turtling'. I was very pleased to see how quickly the children were able to use LOGO; Karen wrote, 'It is easy to learn and does not confuse me'. Christopher commented, 'LOGO is a very good computer language because it does not all have to be learned, because it is made up of the English Language'. Jane explained, 'The turtle uses a very simple language called LOGO. This language includes the easiest of words that are not difficult to remember when you are using the computer'. David wrote, 'My cousin has a ZX 81 and the language we use is Basic but I find the language we use with the turtle (LOGO) is much easier to understand. The turtle also makes you *think* about what you are going to do'.

An example of one of the first pictures drawn was Barry's boat. Barry, age ten, typed in

FORWARD 45
RIGHT 45
FORWARD 10.5
RIGHT 135
FORWARD 7.5
LEFT 45
FORWARD 7
BACKWARD 7
RIGHT 45
FORWARD 40
LEFT 90
FORWARD 7.5
RIGHT 90
FORWARD 5
RIGHT 135
FORWARD 5.25
LEFT 90
FORWARD 5.25
RIGHT 135
FORWARD 5
LEFT 90
FORWARD 10

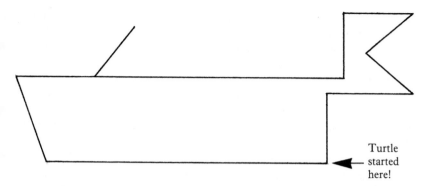

Turtle
started
here!

How did I see the Floor Turtle after such a short use? I found it was something the children could identify with. It moved through space as they did, turning as they did, not like the arrow on the screen (the Screen Turtle) which went up in the air when it went forward, or sideways, or towards the ground! After only a few sessions I could see interesting aspects in the children's work. They began to appreciate using two different measures for length and turning. They were beginning to realize the need to order their thoughts and to plan several moves ahead.

The environment created by the 'Turtle' and the small-group activity encouraged the children to cooperate, to share jobs, discuss ideas with each other, put forward arguments in support of ideas when trying to influence others, make decisions, use logical thinking, analyse mistakes, look for causes of errors and find remedies to correct these in perfecting their programs as they instructed the Floor Turtle to draw. I found them experiencing real problems and often solving them through trial and error. They found the work novel, challenging and absorbing, spending long periods concentrating and persisting with their own ideas. They (not I, the teacher) were initiating the direction of their learning.

Mathematics and the 'Turtle'

A new school year began in September 1981. Then in November it was suggested that I might use the Floor Turtle for a term in my school. So for four months between December 1981 and March 1982 I used the Turtle daily in my normal teaching environment. I normally work with three sets of children for mathematics each morning. They are from the second, third and fourth year Junior age range. The two mixed ability classes from each year group are 'set' for mathematics. The two class teachers and I share the 60 to 70 children accordingly, and work with three groups each daily. I work with the 'least able' second-year children, the 'average' third-year children, and the 'most able' fourth-year group. The second-year group contained 14 children, the third-year group was 30, and the fourth-years were 20.

I was anxious to use the Turtle as a small group activity, so that it would fit into my normal work. I did not want the 'Turtle Group' to take any more of my time than any other activity or group of children in the room. In fact, throughout the term, teacher supervision was minimal. Each session the children 'Turtled' for a whole lesson in their 'Turtle Groups', when it was their group's turn. We saved the work, clipping the pictures on a large easel at the back of the room. Our aim was to let every child in the school 'Turtle'. I took groups of children I do not normally teach in the mornings for Turtle group sessions in the afternoon. This enabled me to spend time listening to the children as they articulated their thoughts and ideas in a real mathematical context, and observing the way they tackled the 'real' problems that the Turtle brought them up against. I became much more aware of my own use of language and was able to analyse my own questioning techniques. I found it very difficult at times not to tell them how to do something; I was learning to keep quiet! I found the children working in open-ended situations and exploring interesting ideas of their own as they arose. They came up against real problems. These had to be identified, analysed and tackled often several ways before a solution could be found. Their drawings were creating problems but the Turtle was giving the children the means of finding solutions.

I was enjoying the bonus of observing the children in situations in which they became totally involved. The problems were created by the children who were thus motivated to seek 'their' solutions. The 'Turtle' environment was providing a 'learning' environment in a wider context than purely mathematics.

Nicolas said, 'We are trying to work out how we can get the Turtle to draw a flat circle to go on our "Pillar Box".' They sat down at the computer and discussed how they would do this. John said, 'We know how to make a circle. We go FORWARD a bit and RIGHT a bit, lots of times. We don't want to go very far round. Shall we try FORWARD 1 and RIGHT 4, for 8 times?' At this stage I was able to show the children a new command that they could give the Turtle. If you want to do a sequence of movements more than once you can use REPEAT. So the boys were able to type in

REPEAT 8
FORWARD 1
RIGHT 4
LIMIT (To mark the end of the repeating sequence)

This produced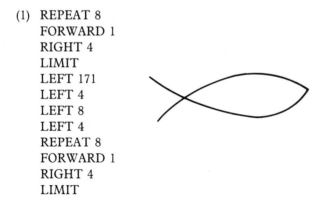

Now they decided to turn the Turtle around so they could come back and reach the starting point with a 'matching half'. After much moving themselves, lining up their bodies with the Floor Turtle, acting out what they thought it would do in response to their commands, they typed RIGHT 175. 'Too much, go LEFT 1, no LEFT 1 more'. After this they felt they would be able to repeat their sequence again and the Turtle would return to its original place.

Now they typed,

REPEAT 8
FORWARD 1
RIGHT 4
LIMIT

The result was

Nicolas commented, 'We need to get the angle right when we turn halfway'. They then continued to try different angles, until eventually the desired shape was achieved.

(1) REPEAT 8
     FORWARD 1
     RIGHT 4
     LIMIT
     LEFT 171
     LEFT 4
     LEFT 8
     LEFT 4
     REPEAT 8
     FORWARD 1
     RIGHT 4
     LIMIT

(2) REPEAT 8
     FORWARD 1
     RIGHT 4
     LIMIT
     RIGHT 167
     LEFT 6
     LEFT 6
     REPEAT 8
     FORWARD 1
     RIGHT 4
     LIMIT

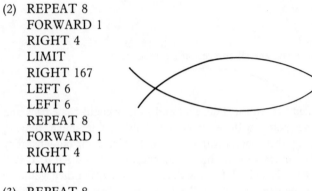

(3) REPEAT 8
     FORWARD 1
     RIGHT 4
     LIMIT
     RIGHT 155
     LEFT 5
     LEFT 1

('I'll try Left 1 for luck', said John.)

   REPEAT 8
   FORWARD 1
   RIGHT 4
   LIMIT

Nicolas remarked 'That means my angle is RIGHT 148 in the middle'.
   A second problem arose now. 'How do we get the size right, now we've got the right shape?' This was their approach to solving that one!
   John said, 'I think, if we double the instructions, I'll get a bigger one. I'll multiply by 4'.

(1) REPEAT 8
     FORWARD 4
     RIGHT 16
     LIMIT
     RIGHT 148
     LEFT 20
     LEFT 20
     LEFT 10

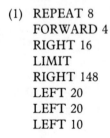

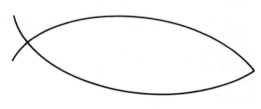

```
LEFT 5
REPEAT 8
FORWARD 4
RIGHT 16
LIMIT
```

'That angle is wrong again in the middle'.

(2)
```
REPEAT 8
FORWARD 4
RIGHT 16
LIMIT
RIGHT 80
LEFT 10
LEFT 5
REPEAT 8
FORWARD 4
RIGHT 4
LIMIT
```

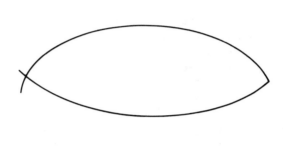

'It's still not right'.

(3)
```
REPEAT 8
FORWARD 4
RIGHT 16
LIMIT
RIGHT 50
REPEAT 8
FORWARD 4
RIGHT 16
LIMIT
```

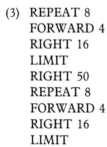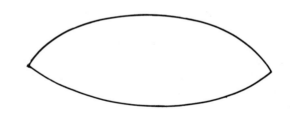

They were than able to go on and draw their pillar box.

As the groups worked, many examples of solving problems were produced and it was now that I could see that they were tackling most by trial and error. They were learning that mistakes didn't matter because they could help you to find the right way to do something. They were practising finding ways to approach problems. They had to identify exactly what the problem was that was causing things to go wrong. All the time they were thinking, evaluating the results of their thoughts, communicating their LOGO ideas to others and making decisions. LOGO was encouraging flexible thinking.

I allowed the children plenty of exploratory time at the beginning. The Floor Turtle's drawing was my (and their) record. I waited for signs that written instructions or pre-planning might be needed. It was not long before children were making little sketches of what they were going to get the Turtle to draw, at the beginning of the session, in the corner of the paper that the Floor Turtle was going to draw on. Then I was asked, 'Can we plan our drawing, so we don't waste any of our time when it's our next turn on the Turtle?' I offered drawing and writing paper. So rough sketches were drawn in advance, and it was not long before lists of instructions, that they would type into the computer to get the Floor Turtle to draw their pictures, were being written in readiness for their next 'Turtle turn'.

Soon the older children were asking for squared and graph paper and circular protractors and making scale drawings. Jonathan wrote, 'My favourite part of Turtle work is simulating how our planning will work before seeing it on the screen and floor'.

After my 'Turtle term' I was convinced that the Turtle was indeed a 'tool to think with'. Logical thinking was needed to analyse mistakes and formulate hypotheses. The children were taking the initiative. They were controlling the robot, not being controlled by it!

As their experience grew, the older children were ready to move on. A group of children asked one day, 'Now we know how to do a shape, we want to do it lots of times, isn't there a way we could tell the Turtle to keep making it, so we don't have to keep typing in all the instructions everytime?' Well, there is! The children were ready to go onto the next stage and learn how to build procedures. Here is an example of making a procedure. A group of girls trying to make a head for their monster had learned that they could make a triangle by typing,

REPEAT 3,
FORWARD 20
LEFT 120

They wanted to make the head hexagonal. So instead of typing the instructions for the triangle six times they learnt how to make a procedure TRI.

The version of LOGO that I have been using is a small subset of LOGO, that enables us to control a Floor Turtle, and at the same time a Screen Turtle, which is an arrow head that moves around the monitor screen, drawing the same pictures as the Floor Turtle. To make a procedure which

can be stored in the computer's memory, such as TRI, you type BUILD
followed by the procedure name. So the girls typed

```
BUILD TRI
REPEAT 3
FORWARD 20
LEFT 120
LIMIT
END.
```

Every time a triangle was needed thereafter, they could type TRI and the
computer would draw one. So to make their hexagon, they typed

```
BUILD HEAD
REPEAT 6
TRI
LIMIT
LEFT 180
END.
```

So the monster's head was made   ⟶

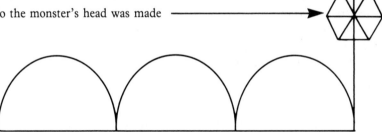

My Turtle term had been great fun. It had convinced me that LOGO had a
place in the Primary school. Every one of the children, all 240 of them
between seven and eleven, had used it, and after four months we had not come
anywhere near the end of its possibilities. The older children had begun to
design their own 'language' to use with the computer, through defining and
using their own procedures and, most importantly, I felt they were learning
how to learn. I very reluctantly returned the Floor Turtle at the beginning of
the Easter holidays.

Further development — beyond mathematics

I was keen to go further with LOGO but had to wait until new software was available to allow me to be able to 'save' the children's procedures between their 'turns', so that they could carry on developing their ideas. The next school year started and by the end of November we acquired our own Floor Turtle. I began using it as before, with new groups of children. By the time the older children were building procedures I had acquired the extra memory space in the computer and the new software that allowed me to 'save' the children's work on cassettes, for reloading in subsequent sessions. I began to use 'ARROW', a program written for RML 480Z and 380Z machines.

As before, the children went through a sequence of exploration just with the Floor Turtle at first, sketching proposed Turtle drawings, making scale drawings, pre-planning their listing of proposed Turtle commands before their turn on the computer. The older children, as their confidence and understanding increased, began turning off the Floor Turtle and focusing their attention on the Screen Turtle.

It began to emerge that there were two approaches. Some groups would create large procedures of such things as animals and approached the idea by trying to make the whole animal as one unit. One such procedure was LEO. LEO was created by a group of girls who created four animals in such a way. This program was typed in and changed many times by the editing facility.

LEO

(1)	(a)	(b)	(c)	(d)
	PEN ON	RIGHT 90	FORWARD 8	RIGHT 90
	RIGHT 90	FORWARD 8	RIGHT 90	FORWARD 8
	FORWARD 40	LEFT 90	FORWARD 24	LEFT 90
	RIGHT 90	FORWARD 8	RIGHT 90	FORWARD 8
	FORWARD 8	RIGHT 90	FORWARD 8	RIGHT 90
	LEFT 90	FORWARD 8	LEFT 90	FORWARD 8
	FORWARD 8	LEFT 90	FORWARD 8	LEFT 90

(2)	(a)	(b)	(c)	(d)
	FORWARD 8	RIGHT 45	FORWARD 24	LEFT 90
	RIGHT 90	FORWARD 12	RIGHT 45	FORWARD 12
	FORWARD 12	RIGHT 45	FORWARD 12	RIGHT 90
	LEFT 90	FORWARD 24	RIGHT 45	FORWARD 8
	FORWARD 8	RIGHT 90	FORWARD 28	LEFT 90
	LEFT 90	FORWARD 96	LEFT 90	
	FORWARD 28	RIGHT 90	FORWARD 8	

(3)	(a)	(b)	(c)	(d)
	FORWARD 8	LEFT 90	FORWARD 8	LEFT 90
	RIGHT 90	FORWARD 8	RIGHT 90	FORWARD 8
	FORWARD 8	RIGHT 90	FORWARD 8	PEN OFF
	LEFT 90	FORWARD 24	LEFT 90	BACKWARD 24
	FORWARD 8	RIGHT 90	FORWARD 8	
	RIGHT 90	FORWARD 8	RIGHT 90	
	FORWARD 8	LEFT 90	FORWARD 8	

(4)	(a)	(b)	(c)	(d)
	RIGHT 90	RIGHT 45	FORWARD 4	PEN ON
	PEN ON	FORWARD 4	RIGHT 45	REPEAT 3
	FORWARD 4	RIGHT 45	FORWARD 4	FORWARD 4
	RIGHT 45	FORWARD 4	PEN OFF	RIGHT 90
	FORWARD 4	RIGHT 45	BACKWARD 4	LIMIT
	RIGHT 45	FORWARD 4	RIGHT 45	FORWARD 4
	FORWARD 4	RIGHT 45	FORWARD 4	PEN OFF

(5)	(a)	(b)	(c)	(d)
	RIGHT 90	PEN OFF	FORWARD 4	PEN ON
	FORWARD 32	RIGHT 45	PEN OFF	REPEAT 3
	LEFT 45	FORWARD 4	LEFT 90	FORWARD 4
	PEN ON	PEN ON	FORWARD 4	RIGHT 90
	REPEAT 8	REPEAT 3	FORWARD 12	LIMIT
	FORWARD 4	FORWARD 4	LEFT 90	FORWARD 4
	RIGHT 45	RIGHT 90	FORWARD 4	RIGHT 45
	LIMIT	LIMIT	LEFT 90	FORWARD 8

(6)	(a)	(b)	(c)	(d)
	REPEAT 2	FORWARD 4	PEN ON	FORWARD 4
	RIGHT 45	RIGHT 90	REPEAT 2	RIGHT 45
	FORWARD 4	FORWARD 4	FORWARD 4	FORWARD 8
	LIMIT	PEN OFF	RIGHT 45	RIGHT 45
	RIGHT 45	RIGHT 90	LIMIT	FORWARD 4
	FORWARD 4	FORWARD 16	FORWARD 8	RIGHT 45
	LEFT 90	LEFT 90	RIGHT 45	FORWARD 8

(7)	(a)
	RIGHT 45
	FORWARD 4
	RIGHT 45
	FORWARD 4
	PEN OFF

LEO

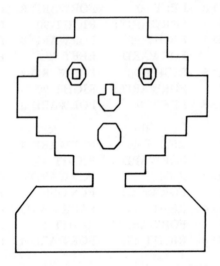

Subsequently I challenged this group to see if they could have found an easier way of drawing their lion, suggesting that they could have done it in parts, by building procedures for the eyes or nose or mouth and so on. Mary agreed that this might be an easier way, but added that they enjoyed doing it 'our way', because, she said, 'It is great fun and a challenge to find the mistakes'.

Other groups of children broke down their problems into parts (sub-problems) and built these up to make a 'whole picture'. An example of this was a DOG drawn by a group of boys. They built up procedures one at a time and put them together as each one worked for them, until they had built DOG.

They defined procedures, FIRST, HEAD, FEN, A, EYES, B, and DOG. 'FIRST' positioned the Turtle to begin drawing. HEAD was made by:

REPEAT 2
RIGHT 45
FORWARD 60
RIGHT 45
FORWARD 30
RIGHT 45
FORWARD 40
RIGHT 45

```
FORWARD 30
LIMIT
END.
```

FEN (Forehead, Ears, Nose) followed!
Then A was defined as,

```
RIGHT 135
HEAD
FEN
END.
```

EYES were made and B was,

```
A
EYES
END.
```

DOG was finished (Figure 5.1) and made from

```
FIRST
B
END.
```

It was not long after this that the children began investigating the idea of
using similar shapes but with different sizes. At this stage it was an ideal
opportunity to introduce the idea of a variable. With our subset of LOGO
('ARROW') we could for instance make a procedure that would draw a
LEAF. A group drawing a flower needed a similar shape for both petals and
leaves in their drawing. They had defined a leaf, as

```
LEAF
REPEAT 13
FORWARD 2
LEFT 4
LIMIT
LEFT 128
REPEAT 13
FORWARD 2
LEFT 4
LIMIT
END.
```

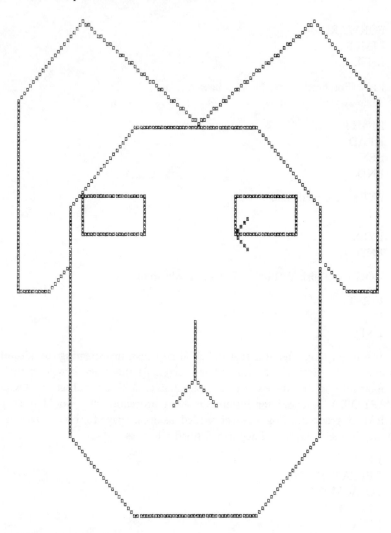

Figure 5.1 Printout of DOG

I was able to show them how to make a leaf that could be used with a different number for the FORWARD instruction so as to change the size of the leaf.

We could BUILD LEAF WITH SIZE (we could choose other names such as LENGTH etc.).

```
REPEAT 13
FORWARD SIZE
LEFT 4
LIMIT
LEFT 128
REPEAT 13
FORWARD SIZE
LEFT 4
LIMIT
END.
```

Each time the children needed the shape drawn they would need only to give the computer the size of the FORWARD movement and type

```
MAKE SIZE BECOME 10
LEAF
```

This would produce a 'petal' size,

Whereas,

```
MAKE SIZE BECOME 20
LEAF
```

would produce a 'leaf' size,

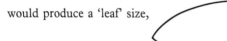

The children spent a long time working on patterns on the screen. An example of a group of boys experimenting was CROSSEYES. Here is their procedure:

```
BUILD CROSSEYES.
CIRCLE
RIGHT 180
CIRCLE
RIGHT 90
CIRCLE
RIGHT 180
CIRCLE
END.
```

Circle had been defined as

```
CIR WITH LENGTH
PEN ON
MAKE LENGTH BECOME 1
REPEAT 72
FORWARD LENGTH
LEFT 5
LIMIT
REPEAT 4
MAKE LENGTH BECOME 1 MORE
REPEAT 72
FORWARD LENGTH
LEFT 5
LIMIT
LIMIT
END.
```

Arithmetic was now being used too! Figure 5.2 shows the printout of CROSSEYES.

Thus the children were able to 'play' with the ideas they had had themselves. Perhaps the success in the classroom is best summed up by the children themselves.

Karen, aged ten, wrote, 'It is fun seeing the Turtle move around the floor. Making procedures is demanding. At first I thought the Turtle was a load of old rubbish but now I have changed my mind completely. I think it has helped me in understanding angles and degrees'.

Peter, aged eleven, saw another aspect in their 'Turtling'. 'Before I started using the Turtle my attitude towards computers was that they were just things that worked out accounts and played games. I feel myself that the Turtle is not just a geometrical robot that draws; it helps children get on with each other as, in using the Turtle, group decisions are vital'.

Rosamund wrote, 'I don't think anyone could *not* learn things from the Turtle. Just sitting at a desk doing sums is not nearly as inspired as the Turtle. You can learn just as much, if not more with the Turtle'.

Jonathan commented, 'The Turtle is very rewarding and when all plans are perfected the excitement builds up and if you could hear the shouts of delight when everything comes out alright'.

Linda, aged eleven, wrote, 'I think the Turtle is good fun, but you also have to do quite a bit of mathematical thinking, so you also learn a lot'.

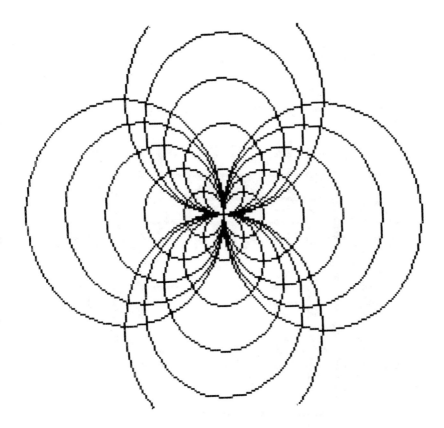

Figure 5.2   Printout of 'Crosseyes'

Phillipa summarized her feelings thus: 'The Turtle is helpful in lots of ways like teaching you angles and degrees. LOGO is simple to learn and can be taught quickly. Lately I have had great fun out of working out what we are going to draw on the Turtle when it is our next turn. It is also fun trying to find out where you have made mistakes (if you do). When you finally get the picture right it is very pleasing and satisfying'.

Perhaps Paul put his finger on its child appeal. 'The Turtle is great to use because you have more freedom than when you work in a book'.

The 'freedom' Paul talked of produced some very interesting ideas, that brought an aesthetic dimension to their mathematics during the later exploratory work. Many examples emerged from the LOGO sessions. Designs with pleasing appearances were produced. Here are two such examples.

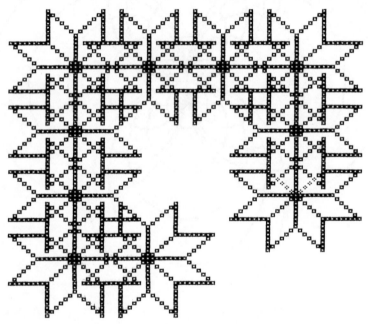

Figure 5.3 'Patty'

The first is 'Patty' (Figure 5.3). Patty was the result of a very simple idea known to the girls who produced it as 'Frisky'. Frisky was a 'Rhombus'. Eight 'Friskies' became 'Snowdrop', and 'Snowdrop', followed by a forward movement and then repeated, became 'Two Snow'. 'Patty' grew from a repeating sequence of 'Two Snow', a turn, and a forward command (Figure 5.4).

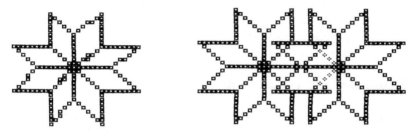

Figure 5.4 'Snowdrop' and 'Two-snow'

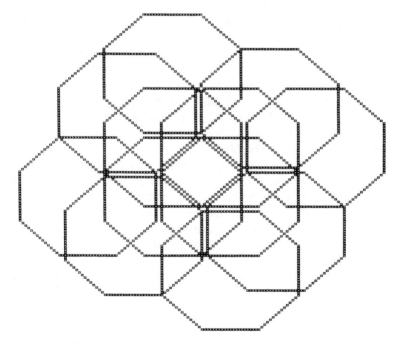

Figure 5.5 'Spinny'

'Spinny' (Figure 5.5) was another result of playing with a simple idea; in this case, an octagon. This produced another satisfying and 'eye-pleasing' shape!

'Oct', the octagon, was followed by turning and forward movements to give 'Tudglee'. The final result, 'Spinny', was a combination of '4 Tudglees'. The children really enjoyed 'choosing' their own names and making the 'language' they were building up, in their procedures, their own personal property. Perhaps there are possibilities of using the 'Turtle graphics' subset of LOGO with young children to encourage interest in design.

Summary and conclusions

So, why LOGO? I really do feel that I have been using that extra potential of the computer. LOGO enables the children themselves to have control over their own learning. It is flexible and so well structured in itself that the children do build on their knowledge as they progress. They experience the 'joy of discovery', and become totally absorbed. They have the freedom to work at their own level and to be in control of the speed and depth of learning. They also begin to get ideas about programming computers through meaningful activity. LOGO has not alienated the children and after nearly six months of continuous use I have not yet been asked, 'Do I have to go on the computer today?' It has made me think very much about the computer as a real learning resource. I believe LOGO gives children a new opportunity. It encourages children to think for themselves, to form opinions and to follow through their own logic. The LOGO environment provides an atmosphere, where they are not frightened to communicate their thinking, be it right or wrong, because they accept that wrong answers can be helpful in learning. They have the opportunity to listen to and question their peers in their own words. Ideas are thus supported and justified and their theories proved or disproved. These are all experiences that help to develop a scientific approach to their learning. They experience 'real problem-solving', with practice in identifying and analysing their problems. They need to find strategies and can consider a variety of approaches. Using the computer in a second-rate role, mimicking other forms of teaching and offering old diets in a novel setting is not for me!

CHAPTER 6

MICROS AND MATHEMATICAL THINKING

CHARLES BAKE

Britain will be the first country in the world to have microcomputers in every Secondary and Primary school. The DOI has funded 50 per cent of each microcomputer bought through the government scheme while the MEP's training programme for teachers will have cost around £20 million by 1986. Schools themselves are spending hundreds of pounds on software and peripherals — not to mention their share of the cost of each micro they buy. But is it all worth while? Garland (1982, p.1) makes the point that, 'Education is filled with the traces and the ghosts of ideas and ideals that blazed into prominence like some super-nova and then burnt themselves out, leaving only a wisp of their previous glory. It could be that the same will happen in the case of using microcomputers in our teaching with primary-aged children'. Will educationalists of years to come see the advent of the micro as a new, exciting turning point in the direction of education or as an expensive folly? Already, as David Dodds pointed out in Chapter 3, serious doubts have been expressed about the whole enterprise. An article in the *Observer* (24 October 1982) reported the fears of computer advisers that insufficient training coupled with a lack of good software would be highly detrimental to pupils: Primary education could be set back some twenty years! I do not share that pessimistic view though I do argue against the over-use of drill programs as I feel this is a narrow use of an exciting resource. I see micros as providing a new dimension to the Primary school curriculum and helping teachers to develop their pupils' thinking ability. In this chapter, I want to explore some of the uses to which micros can be put in Primary schools to assist the teaching of mathematics. In particular I will point to the links between certain programs and the development of mathematical thinking providing illustrative examples of my own uses of micros (and Bigtrak) with Junior and Infant pupils at Woodside School in Croydon. I want to start, however, by giving a flavour of the sort of use to which a computer can be put by showing how it can extend the scope of mathematical topics: in this instance, the sorting and classification of sets.

Sorting data

My approach to using a micro for this extension work in mathematics was greatly influenced by the experiences of Frank Gregory (Mathematics and Computing Adviser for the Isle of Wight). Briefly, for those who do not know of his work, he describes (Gregory 1983) how he used a six-line BASIC program with Middle school children to sort data — in this case information about an imaginary crime. In addition to using this program he also used punched cards to demonstrate to the children how they could sort the relevant data about the 'suspects' and obtain the same answers as the computer. The point of this was to demystify data handling and show how a computer sifted through the data by simply making choices between alternatives.

This seemed a novel way of extending work I was carrying out into sets. Initially I wondered whether I should try to show the power of a computer by using a proprietary data handling program such as FACTFILE. So I decided to try out FACTFILE for myself. However, I rejected it on the grounds that it did not seem powerful enough to me — ten fields would limit the number of entries to 25* pupils. If at some future date I wanted to introduce the children to a genuine data handling program then I would select one that could sort a lot of information and thereby demonstrate how powerful an aid a micro could be. In addition (and this to me seemed more important), it reinforced the 'black box' image of the micro — out would pop the answers to a query as if by magic — something I have always tried to avoid when using a micro with children. So I took Frank Gregory's ideas on board.

At the time my class was engaged on a topic about the Romans and we had just begun to deal with the life of Julius Caesar. His ultimate assassination and the hunt for those responsible seemed a possible subject for me on which to try out Gregory's ideas. Each child in the class devised a Roman name for himself or herself — Helena, Billius and the like. Then we discussed what sorts of information might have come to light following Caesar's murder, given that the assailants were unknown. Various ideas were forwarded on

*On correct version of FACTFILE the limit has been increased to 47 pupils.

those physical characteristics which might help identify the culprits and after further discussion a final list of fields was agreed upon:

— was the assassin a man?
— was he/she tall?
— did he/she have brown hair?
— did the murderer drive a chariot?
— was the assassin wearing a red toga?
— did he/she have a gold brooch?
— was the murderer carrying a sword?
— did he/she have a scar?
— or a tattoo (!)?
— and, finally, was he/she seen at the Forum on the Ides of March?

Each child then decided what particular attributes his/her Roman *alter ego* would possess. This information was filled in on punched cards as shown in Figure 6.1. If a child answered 'yes' to one of the questions then a hole would be cut away: if 'no' then the space was left intact.

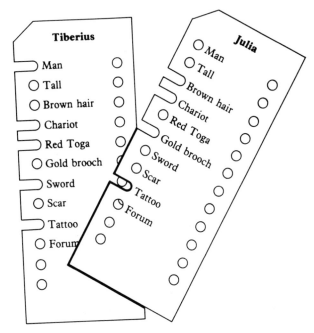

Figure 6.1   Punched cards

I then demonstrated to my class how punched cards could be used to sift through the information about the possible suspects. For example, supposing we wanted to see which Roman women were wearing a red toga on the day of the murder. Once the cards had been stacked together a needle could be placed through the holes and slits of question A 'Are you a man?' By lifting the needle, those cards with a slit next to question A (i.e. those children who had answered 'yes') would fall through and those left pierced by the needle would be the 'Roman women'. This pile of cards could then be sorted a second time by placing the needle through the holes adjacent to question E. This time those cards with a slit (i.e. 'Yes. They were wearing a red toga') would fall out and be the ones we needed. I got each child to try several such sorts just to see how the system worked.

The next step was to introduce the class to the BASIC program that they would be using. I had adapted Frank Gregory's six-line program and, as can be seen, I had five rather than six lines in the main body of the program (lines 10 to 50).

```
10 CLS
20 FOR suspect = 1 TO 23
30 READ name$, A,B,C,D,E,F,G,H,I,J
40 IF A =1 AND C = 0 AND H = 1 THEN PRINT name$
50 NEXT suspect
60 DATA Celia, 0,0,1,1,0,0,0,1,0,1
70 DATA Billius, 1,0,0,0,1,1,1,0,1,0
80 DATA Silvia, 0,1,1,0,0,1,1,0,0,0
```

and so on.

Each child then had to type in his or her own line of data — not an easy process when the slightest error in syntax would make the program crash. As can be seen from the program each line contained the Roman name then a series of 1s and 0s. These corresponded with the holes ('Noes') and slits ('Yeses') on the punched cards. The children were therefore able to transfer their 'Yes' and 'No' responses from the cards to the BASIC program quite easily and were encouraged to cross-check one against the other when they had finished. So after a couple of hours, all the lines of data had been incorporated into the program.

I had already secretly decided upon the identity of the two murderers and had used the punched cards myself to work out which characteristics each possessed. The children would have to work out who the culprits were on the basis of the evidence I gave them. Initially I told the children that the Roman authorities already knew that a man and a woman had been seen behaving suspiciously and that the man was short while the woman was of medium height. This information was used to sort the punched cards using plastic needles. The same data were also typed in to alter line 40 of the BASIC program accordingly (i.e. 40 IF A = 0 AND G = 1 THEN PRINT name$). When the program was run the names of current suspects were printed on the screen and the children could see that they matched those of the punched cards they had already sorted out.

Over the next few days other information leading to the identity of Caesar's murderers was discovered by the children — I left anonymous notes and clues hidden around the classroom and waited until someone stumbled across them. Sometimes the children would turn to the micro first in order to see which suspects had now been eliminated, while at other times they used the punched cards first. This was largely dependent upon the current availability of the micro. As part of this work each child wrote a 'Roman newspaper' and told of the latest developments in the hunt for the assassins. Eventually the culprits, Billius and Livia, were unmasked and suffered a horrible fate.

Mathematics lessons

Apart from its use in large projects like that given above a micro also has a place in day-to-day mathematics lessons.

Paragraph 243 of the Cockcroft Report (DES 1982) says that mathematics teaching should include opportunities for the following six features:

1. exposition by the teacher:
2. discussion between teacher and pupils and between pupils themselves:
3. appropriate practical work:
4. consolidation and practice of fundamental skills and routines:
5. problem-solving, including the application of mathematics to everyday situations:
6. investigational work.

1: The exposition by a teacher of a new concept can be greatly facilitated through the use of a micro in its role as an animated blackboard. By this I mean that the teacher can use the micro to introduce a topic by displaying, say, diagrams or number sequences on the monitor rather than by using structural apparatus or writing on the blackboard or the OHP. While these latter methods may prove adequate for the exposition of most mathematical topics some computer software can offer a fresh approach and introduce a new dimension to mathematics. One such program is TAKE HALF. It takes the form of an 11-minute 'film' and shows a square continually being divided in half through increasingly complex kaleidoscope-type patterns. This is clearly something which a teacher could not demonstrate to the same degree of complexity in any other way and would make a stimulating starting point for children to explore the concept of fractions.

2:   A microcomputer can certainly initiate much lively discussions between children — a fact borne out by anyone who has used a micro with a group of children. My Case Studies below give instances of this in the work I have undertaken with the children at Woodside.

3:   A computer can also be the starting point for practical work away from the machine itself. For example, the program EUREKA, which I discuss below, is concerned with the displacement of water and would serve as a launching pad for investigations into the volume of everyday objects using the displacement method.

4:   For many teachers, however, the link between microcomputers and mathematics centres on point 4 — the practice of skills and regular use of drill programs. This link between drill programs and mathematics extends to so-called 'educational' software produced for schools and the home computer market. This seems to concentrate solely on this type of program. Typical are those drill programs designed to help children learn multiplication tables. Such programs may dress these activities up in the guise of car races (where refuelling the car depends on the pupil giving the correct answer to a multiplication question) or may reward the pupil's ability to perform a simple calculation by flashing a smiling face on the monitor screen or by playing a catchy tune — yet drill exercises they remain. They may keep a child happily occupied for half an hour or so but do they teach him anything in the full sense? And, what is the benefit of using a micro for this type of activity over using, say, a more traditional approach such as a flashcard game? It is of course the case that a micro can often motivate children to concentrate harder and perhaps to perform better than when using workcards. Also, drill programs allow the child to work at his/her own pace and they are self-correcting in that they will usually provide the correct answer to a question if a wrong answer is typed in. But it should not be automatically assumed that these are always advantages. The quality of the learning experience must always be the prime consideration.

Why then should this use of a micro prove so attractive to many teachers? I think that to a large extent the answer lies in their attitudes towards the new technology and in the consequent problems which Leslie Smith discussed in Chapter 2.

Not all teachers have welcomed the arrival of a microcomputer in their school. As Chapter 2 explained, many have felt themselves under threat by machines which they do not readily understand yet which the pupils seem to take to easily. A micro can upset the *status quo* of the classroom and the teacher may feel that his authority — and by that I mean 'superior know-how' — is being undermined if the pupils seem to know more about the micro than he does. Thus a computer can be the catalyst that promotes a subtle shift in the power-base in the classroom from a teacher-dominant situation to one in which the pupils begin to direct the curriculum for themselves and where the teacher may have to turn to the pupil to seek guidance on how to use the micro.

Many teachers who fear this change oppose the use of micros in their classroom. There are also those teachers who remain unconvinced of the value of a micro yet somewhat reluctantly agree to use it — perhaps hoping that its inadequacies will be exposed by them so they can say 'I told you so'. Sometimes negative attitudes towards the micro manifest themselves in its use as a time-filler which has little contribution to make to the 'real' work of the class. The instruction 'When you've finished your work you can go and use the micro' is something I have heard more than once. Much of the distrust of teachers for the new technology stems from their being unsure how to operate the machines properly themselves, and knowing what to do when a program crashes or the micro fails to respond as expected. This does little to help a teacher already lacking in confidence when confronted with a micro and is likely to be an important contributory consideration to him in deciding whether to try to use the machine or ignore it.

Such teachers are unlikely to be adventurous in their choice of software: they will probably look for those programs of a straightforward type where they will need to intervene as little as possible. Drill programs fit the bill admirably. For they are not difficult to learn how to use. They allow the teacher to organize the class so that individual children follow some rota system and sit at the micro, LOAD whatever program they require and RUN it. Then when they have finished they simply inform the next pupil that it is his/her turn to use the machine. Thus there is the minimum disruption to the work of the rest of the class. This kind of use, however, brings about no significant change of approach to the curriculum and, as was stressed in Chapter 1, it fails to tap the educational potential which the advent of the micro offers.

The popularity of this use of a computer is reflected in the fact that even the first audio cassette tape of the Micro Primer pack (a package which accompanies each micro bought under the DOI scheme and which is designed for distance study by teachers unfamiliar with micros) devotes much time to giving examples of just such uses of micros by teachers in the North of England. The over-use of drill programs seems to me to be leading to the micro being used as an expensive teaching machine to which only one pupil is exposed at a time.

To counteract this approach teachers should be able to handle micros with confidence. However, the MEP-run in-service training is hardly up to the job. What can two teachers from each school hope to learn even with two full days' training? Will the rest of the staff see them as 'experts' and, upon finding that they are not, deem micros as too complicated and lose all interest themselves in micros?

Similarly, if the children are not to be frustrated in their desire to use the micro it is important that they should know how to use micros properly: how to set up the equipment and LOAD and RUN programs for themselves. They are not likely to be able to use a micro for their purposes and do so confidently and successfully if they are fearful of damaging the machine or if they get disheartened by being unable to make it work. So they must be explicitly taught how to use the micro too. At my school I have been doing precisely this with a group of children who attend a lunchtime computer club. They have been learning how to set up the micro, how to LOAD and SAVE programs and how to handle those problems that occur (e.g. if the program fails to LOAD or the program is temporarily 'lost' when the Reset button has been pressed). In addition we have spent much time talking about micros and trying to clarify what all the jargon means (ROM, RAM, peripherals etc.). The framework for this exercise derives from a scheme currently being developed in Croydon by Trisha Strong, whereby children work towards progressively more demanding levels of a Certificate in Computer Competence. This is part of a broader project at Croydon to develop resource materials for the study of Information Technology.

Now I am not saying that the use of drill programs is to be avoided at all costs. Children do need to practise skills if they are to internalize them and a micro can provide endless repetitive exercises without becoming bored or losing its temper. It is a neutral arbiter and programs can be tailored to allow particular children to work at their own pace and at their own level. However I am arguing that the limitation of micros to drill exercises alone is a waste of an exciting resource. Furthermore, drill programs seldom lend themselves to opportunities for the development of and experimentation with language patterns — so essential to the acquisition of new concepts.

5 and **6**: Cockcroft's other points, problem-solving and investigational work are those areas where I think a microcomputer can prove of most use as they can foster communication and cooperation between children. Group work does encourage communication and cooperation between the children. Admittedly there is the danger that, unless closely monitored, the chidren's conversations will degenerate into aimless chatter, but it is only through opportunities to try to put their thoughts into words that children can grasp and refine concepts.

However, what does not appear in the list of Cockcroft's six points is how a micro can help in the development of mathematical thinking skills themselves.

Micros and thought processes

The idea that a micro can assist children's developing thought processes leads us away from the utilitarian approach of drill programs (where the focus is on the learning of skills and facts) towards a process approach to the curriculum.

Under this view it is the intrinsic values of the experiences that a child has in the classroom that are important rather than the end product of a particular skill having being acquired or certain facts having being memorized. Blenkin and Kelly (1981, p.89) say that a process view implies that the curriculum be 'defined in terms of intellectual development and cognitive functioning rather than in terms of quantities of knowledge absorbed or changes of behavioural performance'. A teacher sharing this view of the curriculum would therefore be looking for programs that foster qualitative changes in a child's thinking processes. Drill programs do not meet this requirement.

Developing mathematical thinking

When children acquire new concepts in mathematics they go through a sequence of thought processes: SPECIALIZING, GENERALIZING, CONJECTURING and VERIFYING.

First of all the child tries out particular instances of a new concept (SPECIALIZING). This may involve the ordering, counting, measuring or weighing of objects in the immediate environment or perhaps the manipulation of numbers or geometrical shapes on paper. In other words this is the level at which a child is 'doing'. As stated earlier thought processes are carried out through the medium of language, either silently in one's head or by means of overt communication between people. Thus it is important that at this stage the 'doing' is accompanied by the development of appropriate language with which to describe and refine the mathematical concepts. The advantage for the teacher in encouraging the children to talk about what they are doing is that he can monitor their thought processes and himself inject new ideas. Also when children work together as part of a group ideas are exchanged between them and insights, rather like 'infectious diseases', are spread among the group members.

Secondly the child starts to build up a sense of a general pattern that is common to all of these instances (GENERALIZING). Thus he may see that such diverse activities as potato printing, the counting of centimetre squares within the given pattern and the calculation of the amount of floor space in a room are all particular examples of the general concept of Area.

Thirdly he evolves some idea of what might thus occur in similar, though as yet untried, instances (CONJECTURING). For example, a child may try to guess the next numbers in a given sequence or may be able to extrapolate values from a graph.

Finally he checks whether his CONJECTURES were indeed valid (VERIFYING). This may be achieved by returning to actual examples to see whether a paper and pencil CONJECTURE works in real life; or it may necessitate the use of a general algebraic formula to check that a supposed pattern does in fact hold good over a broad range of values.

A microcomputer can assist children to acquire each of these processes. It can offer the child any number of examples of a particular concept (SPECIALIZATION) from which he can attempt to GENERALIZE an underlying concept. Furthermore it can enable a child to make CONJECTURES and VERIFY them. For example a child can type what he believes to be, say, the next number in a pattern (CONJECTURING) and then, on pressing the RETURN or ENTER key, can discover whether that CONJECTURE was valid or not; the micro will tell him whether his guess was correct or not (VERIFICATION).

I now turn to a number of Case Studies which illustrate the role of a microcomputer in fostering the development of mathematical thinking. First I will describe how I developed a theme of work with Infant children which stemmed from my use of BIGTRAK. Then I will point to other computer programs I have used with Juniors.

Infants and micros

Little work with micros seems to have been undertaken so far by Infant children. Indeed it has been argued (Holloway 1982) that Infant teachers should rather concern themselves with pre-computer 'skills' (keyboard training, the use of various audio-visual aids and the like) in preparation for the children using a micro in the Junior school. However I have found that Infants are perfectly capable of using a microcomputer. Moreover, such training, useful though it may be, seems redundant since Junior children soon seem to acquire the necessary 'skills' to use a micro anyway. It is also a prime example of that tendency to isolate and decontextualize the teaching of 'skills' which almost every contributor to this book has deplored.

The staff of the Infant Department at Woodside were most keen when I suggested that they bring groups of children over to me for forty minutes or so during the dinner breaks in order to use the computer. I had originally intended to set the children working on LOGO straight away. However I decided to start by letting them program something concrete — BIGTRAK — rather than confront them with the abstraction of moving a screen pen (no Floor Turtle being available).

Case study: BIGTRAK

Of the chip-controlled toys around at the minute the one which seems to me to offer most educationally is BIGTRAK. This is a programmable 'tank' which will remember a series of instructions keyed in at a calculator-type pad on the back of the toy. The instructions tell BIGTRAK to move forwards and backwards, turn (up to a full 360°) and repeat instructions if required. It's great fun to play with and has an obvious attraction for young children as it trundles around the floor beeping and flashing.

I had already used BIGTRAK with the lower Junior children in my class, allowing the children to play with the toy — make up routes for themselves and see if they could make BIGTRAK negotiate them. But with the Infants time was indeed limited and there was the consideration that the Infant staff were giving up part of their dinner break to see BIGTRAK in action so that they could evaluate its potential. So this time I tried a different approach by structuring the children's investigations with BIGTRAK. I devised two sorts of activities. The first used small domino-type cards on which I had written various instructions that could be programmed into BIGTRAK (see Figure

Figure 6.2   Instruction cards for BIGTRAK

6.2). The idea was that the children should pick, say, half a dozen of these cards, arrange them in a sequence and then estimate where they thought BIGTRAK would end up.

Figure 6.3 Instructions for BIGTRAK

Having marked that point, the toy was programmed and set in motion. If BIGTRAK did not reach the point that the children had expected then they were invited to suggest alterations to the instructions.

The other activity involved the children being challenged to make BIGTRAK move in a certain pattern across the floor or reach some given objective (see Figure 6.3). This time the children would write down the instructions they thought they needed before they keyed them in. Thus they had a written 'program' and could make any necessary amendments to it if BIGTRAK failed to perform as required.

Several points emerged from the half-dozen sessions I held with the Infants. First of all the children displayed immense concentration and determination — they would have worked on even without the presence of any teachers and were often most reluctant to leave for their dinner sitting. Secondly, the children were confronted with the problems of measuring and talking about space, linear distance and angles. Initially the children needed to experiment with BIGTRAK to see how it performed. For example it was not immediately apparent to them that the units used in the instruction 'FORWARD 3' were BIGTRAK lengths. Similarly when the children first attempted to turn BIGTRAK they were unaware that the turns were given in minute divisions on a clockface. (Thus LEFT 15 would give a quarter-turn to the left: RIGHT 30 a half-turn clockwise.) It was by trial and error that the Infants learnt that turns of 15 or so (depending on the amount of friction between the wheels of BIGTRAK and the surface of the floor) would give the quarter-turn they required. So as the children were initially inputting values less than 10 their attempts at turning BIGTRAK were not very successful.

My role during their work lay in prompting the children to experiment for themselves. Sometimes a suggestion would be forwarded by one of the children and the others would look in my direction, no doubt hoping I would say whether the idea would work or not. On those occasions I put the responsibility for thinking back on the children by asking, 'Well, what do you think about it?' Typical of the children's comments were: 'How far do you think it'll go?'; 'It didn't turn far enough'; 'We want to make it turn this way' (motioning clockwise with the hands).

Lastly the children were engaged in debugging their instructions — an exercise that would recur when using the micro programs CRASH and LOGO. This required them to monitor the progress of BIGTRAK as it moved over the floor and if it failed to perform as expected then decide at what point in the program of instructions an alteration was to be made.

As regards the four components of the mathematical thinking framework listed above, the children were SPECIALIZING (typing in different values for turns and distances); GENERALIZING (gauging how BIGTRAK could be expected to perform, given certain instructions); CONJECTURING (trying to guess which combination of instructions would make BIGTRAK reach a given destination or follow a predetermined path) and VERIFYING (putting BIGTRAK on the classroom floor and seeing how successfully it had been programmed). This type of activity seemed to me to reflect the process approach to education in that the end result of making BIGTRAK move from A to B was not of prime importance. What mattered was that the children were being made to think and to develop various mathematical and linguistic skills. I now wanted to see which computer programs would also encourage this sort of development.

Case study: CRASH

From BIGTRAK I introduced the children to CRASH — a program from the software packs supplied with the DOI micro. This program presents a sort of screen version of BIGTRAK and provided a bridge between the work with BIGTRAK and that with LOGO. In CRASH you have to type out a program of instructions in order to make an arrow move over a grid, avoiding obstacles so as to reach a target area. If the arrow fails to reach the target or if it crashes into one of the obstacles then you can 'debug' the original program with a view to achieving a more successful result. It was this feature of CRASH that I wanted the children to experience as it would provide useful background experience when they came to debugging their procedures with LOGO.

The program certainly proved popular with the Infants and it did not take them long to get the hang of it since the general objective of the game and the instructions themselves were not too dissimilar from their recent experiences with BIGTRAK. As with BIGTRAK the children were engaged with the measurement of angles — although this time as multiples of 45° turns — and distance, though with CRASH they were dealing with screen measurements rather than real-life distances across the floor of the classroom. In addition there were similar opportunities for the children to engage in mathematical thought as with BIGTRAK (e.g. SPECIALIZING by trying the program out: CONJECTURING which commands were necessary to make the arrow avoid a given obstacle, and so on).

Case study: LOGO

As the final activity for the Infants I chose LOGO Challenge, produced by Heather Govier and Malcolm Neave at Croydon. This is by no means a 'full' LOGO — it simply exploits Turtle graphics — but, as Heather Govier (1983, p.11) has pointed out, 'For LOGO to be a valuable tool for learning in the Primary school it need not have all the sophistication of full LOGO such as recursion — a concept much too difficult for most children under twelve'. With LOGO Challenge the children can SPECIALIZE — drawing various shapes, trying different turns etc. — then GENERALIZE — e.g. building up a concept of a right angle or an obtuse angle — then CONJECTURE — think how they might attempt to draw a given design, then VERIFY their plans by typing in the commands at the micro and seeing if in fact they produce the shapes that were intended. It can take teachers some time to get used to the LOGO commands and it was remarkable how quickly the Infants learnt how to use them. By the end of just two half-hour sessions using the micro the Infants were able to draw a square using a REPEAT loop.

As with BIGTRAK and CRASH the hardest part for the children was in deciding on the amount of turn when drawing their shapes. When they first tried to draw a square the general consensus of opinion among the children was that a turn of something under 10 was required. This was not enough. Turns of 50, 80 and 100 were then tried and then one boy suggested the difference be split between 80 and 100 — a turn of 90 proved what was wanted. The children had 'discovered' a right angle.

Junior and micros

I now turn to those programs I have used with Juniors which can contribute to work designed to foster mathematical thinking in children.

Case study: RHINO

A good example of the type of program that can do this is RHINO. In this game an 8 × 8 grid is drawn on the screen. This grid is meant to represent a plan view of the streets of New York. Somewhere on those streets a rhinoceros is hiding — no doubt having escaped from the zoo. By inputting co-ordinates for intersections of particular 'blocks' the children have to locate the rhino. If the co-ordinates they type in are incorrect then the micro tells them how many blocks they must walk in order to reach the rhino. After a number of guesses the possible locations of the rhino diminish.

When children are using this program they are involved in using all of the four aspects of the framework: they SPECIALIZE by typing in particular co-ordinates; they build up experience through this and are then able to GENERALIZE and get an overall view of the game and its strategy; they make CONJECTURES as to where they think the rhino is and then receive VERIFICATION from the micro as to whether their guess was correct or not.

Case study: RAY BOX

This program, which is currently being tested by various schools in the Croydon area, is based on the idea of firing rays into a box in which are hidden a number of atoms. By interpreting what happens to the rays after they have entered the box — whether they are absorbed, reflected or deflected — it is possible to deduce where the atoms must be. Although the concepts of rays and atoms are hardly familiar ones in Primary schools the fact that the children may not be sure precisely what an atom is does not really matter. What is important is that they are involved with acquiring evidence from firing in rays and then making sensible CONJECTURES on the basis of that evidence. So far I have only used this program with second- and third-year Juniors.

Case study: EUREKA

This program is designed to assist children's ability to understand the graphical representation of events. In this instance the screen display is divided into halves. The top portion shows a bath which can be filled and emptied by turning on a tap and removing the plug. A man can be made to get into the bath, thus causing the level of the water to rise, and then get out — having the opposite effect. The bottom portion of the screen displays a line graph which is constantly being updated according to whether the bath is being filled, emptied or whether the man is in or out of the bath. The graph thus shows a gradual incline as it empties. If the man sits in the bath the graph rises sharply to indicate the sudden rise in the level of the water. Both parts of the screen can be displayed simultaneously, or either one at a time. Thus it provides opportunities for the teacher to hide the bottom half of the screen, fill the bath and make the man get in and out then ask the children what sort of graph would they expect to be produced. Alternatively the graph section alone can be shown so that the children are challenged to interpret a given sequence of rises, falls and plateaux on the graph and say what was happening to the bath at the time — was it being filled, when did the man get in, etc?

From the point of view of developing mathematical thinking EUREKA again offers many possibilities for CONJECTURING — asking the children what they think may be happening if the graph is such and such a shape and for VERIFYING, where the other half of the screen can be revealed and the whole sequence of actions replayed to show the children whether their CONJECTURES were right or not.

Summary and conclusions

The support to mathematics provided by micros has been the subject of a recently published discussion paper by an HMI. In *Microcomputers and Mathematics in Schools* T.J. Fletcher (1983) makes a number of points which echo my own experience with microcomputers. He asserts, for example, that young Juniors and Infants can operate the machines — something I discovered in my work with top Infants and lower Juniors. Also he counsels a cautious approach to using micros for the practice of drill. The latter, he argues, needs to be built on previous knowledge and applied in a variety of contexts. Sometimes drill programs are divorced from any context and rely on various rewards to inject enthusiasm into the children. Moreover Fletcher points out that drill programs do not allow a teacher to diagnose problems and therefore must be used with discrimination by the teacher to ensure they match a child's level of competence. A possible avenue to be explored with micros according to Fletcher is through work with a 'rich but restricted language' — by this I imagine he is thinking of LOGO. The joy associated with investigations using BIGTRAK are also noted.

I have myself pointed to similar views of the use of micros and have sought to demonstrate how a micro can assist children in the fundamental task of acquiring the habits of mathematical thinking. Microcomputers can provide pupils with opportunities for investigative group-work and can allow them to discover fundamental mathematical truths for themselves. It is to this use of a microcomputer rather than drill and practice programs that I think teachers should turn.

CHAPTER 7

MICROCOMPUTERS IN SECONDARY EDUCATION — A PERSPECTIVE WITH PARTICULAR REFERENCE TO THE HUMANITIES

DERYN WATSON

It is clear that much attention has been paid in the last few years to the advent of micros in Secondary education. At a time of economic recession this has caused anger among some who see the 'machine' gaining an unfair proportion of the attention and budget of educational administrators. 'A hectic·dash into the new age of information technology, a breathless rush in which it seems that education lacks the wind to dissent' (Webster and Robins 1983). Others have viewed the situation with cynical detachment, aligning themselves with the view that like all fads, the bubble will soon burst. From the perspective of a teacher who has been actively engaged in the research and development of educational software for some time, I will attempt to examine this situation by reflecting on the current and potential educational use of computers, with particular reference to a broad sweep of subjects known as the Humanities, which for the purposes of this chapter, I am referring to as History, Geography, Economics, English and Foreign Languages. This is an area that has received less attention than the sciences (Rushby 1981) or mathematics and computer studies (Howe and Ross 1982). Nevertheless, the Computers in the Curriculum Project, based at Chelsea College (funded by the Schools Council and Microelectronics Education Programme) has been involved in the production of educational software for both the sciences and Humanities since 1973. It is from my involvement in this Project that my views on software for the Humanities are formed, and thus I have used, on the whole, Project software to illustrate my points.

The appearance of micros in schools

At the beginning of this decade it was estimated that 5 per cent of all Secondary schools had access to some form of computing power, via a batch service or telephone line. A mere three years later the Minister for Technology (Baker 1983) reported that every Secondary school in the country had an average of 4.2 micros. Recent conversations between the author and teachers from the Outer London boroughs have given meat to such an average; one school had 16 machines, the other one. Despite such discrepancies, which will have a significant influence on use, to be able to claim that every school has at least one computer is interesting. Can we be sure that every Secondary school has a tape recorder or a set of meteorological thermometers? What is it that makes the micro so special that a Minister for the Department of Industry instigates a scheme to ensure its presence in all schools (Department of Industry 1981)?

The answer is not totally related to education. The Ministry has been concerned to promote British-built micros and accompanying software, and there can be no doubt that the 'micros in schools' scheme is only one small part of an overall thrust of the department in the wake of the then Prime Minister's statements in 1978. '1978 has proved to be the year in which Britain woke up to microelectronics . . . our success will depend upon whether we can adopt this new technology fast enough' (Callaghan 1978). Nevertheless the parallel project run by the Department of Education and Science, the Microelectronics Education Programme (MEP) played a significant role in requesting that hardware should be made available in every school. Without access to hardware, all initiatives with respect to educational computing became meaningless, and yet it is often heard that the reasons there are now micros in schools are unrelated to education.

Examination of the strategy document for the MEP (Fothergill 1981) refutes this claim. The aims of the programme are clear: 'To help schools prepare children for life in a society in which devices and systems based on microelectronics are commonplace and pervasive' (Fothergill 1981, p.1). Like the 'micros in schools' scheme, these aims reflect a combination of concerns and motivations. Thus the practical — all pupils leaving school should be aware of the role and capabilities of computers that they will meet in the adult world — rubs shoulders with a narrower educational definition — all pupils should be given the opportunity to expand their learning horizons through the use of educational software. The three pressures on the system, political, technological and social (Rushby 1979) have all played their part. I intend to leave aside the growth and role of computer studies as well as the use of the computer to manage learning, or even as an aid in the administrative tasks and headaches of a Secondary school. The focus of the question at stake appears to me to be centred on the interrelationship of educational software and the learning operation.

Classroom organization

Examination of the micro's use cannot take place in a false world; the average classroom in the Secondary school still contains 25–30 pupils with one teacher, whose responsibility is confined to a particular discipline base within a set time period. The organization of a micro that can be possible in such an environment has been the subject of some discussion. Shepherd et al. (1980) refer to four models of student–teacher relationship within one classroom, and address themselves to the issue of how large groups of students can use one computer. The models range from the position of the tutor acting as a *gatekeeper* between the students and the computer, the computer acting as a *barrier* between the students and tutor, the *diversionary* in which the students may exclude the tutor, and the *partnership*. This model is possibly more related to the Tertiary rather than the Secondary world. Maddison (1982) devotes a whole chapter to the electronic blackboard as a classroom aid whereby the moving screen becomes an extension of a tool all educators have at some stage used.

The program EUREKA is an excellent example of software designed for the electronic blackboard. The pupils watch a man in a bath, and have to translate such points as filling in the bath, stopping the water when the man gets in, etc. into a line graph of water height. It is clear in screen presentation and designed deliberately for the teacher to drive the program on a large screen with the whole class involved.

The whole class does not however have to be focused on the computer at the same time. In many classes, particularly in science laboratories, a circus of activities is organized around which groups of pupils move.

Nevertheless, such issues highlight the very real problems of organization that Secondary teachers feel they face. Primary teachers are more frequently handling a diversity of activities, and are often in an environment which encourages such a diversity. They may also work in significant time blocks; a Secondary teacher does not normally have more than a single (30–40 minute) or possibly double period at his disposal during which a combination of activities can be executed. The Secondary teacher may feel handicapped when attempting to use the micro in the classroom; such organizational issues may dominate their thinking of the potential and will certainly influence their eagerness to experiment.

The first school I taught in had a raked lecture theatre into which the class would move to view a film. The 16 mm projector was operated by a technician, and the film ordered some while in advance from a commercial supplier. Removing the pupils from the environment of the geography room meant that the film's content was viewed in isolation from other resources and in a relatively inhibiting environment. In four years I can count the number of films I used in single digits. My second school forced me to reassess the position; not only were three 16 mm projectors available to the department, but all were on trolleys and all classrooms had blackout facilities. A regular film library service was operated by the authority with deliveries of up to six films per week. Geographical film became an integrated part of my teaching; the organizational issues no longer dominated and the environment for its use was now educational.

Hence the matter of the physical availability of the micro within the building is another one that may obscure the real issues at stake. Should the teacher be expected to take a class to a computer room or laboratory? Echoes of the constraints caused by language laboratories abound. Micros are highly portable and robust; trolleys may be easily purchased. But myths can hold sway, from the dangers of carrying equipment up stairs to the need for controlled air environments to avoid chalk dust. Most of these positions have absolutely nothing to do with educational computing but a lot to do with the politics of resource and, in particular, micro management within a school.

Nevertheless because such issues are very real at the moment — how many micros live in the Computer Studies cupboard compared with the English cupboard? — the average Secondary school teacher is faced with two major organizational constraints (one teacher per 30 pupils, and 'where is the micro'?) which may act as inhibitors to their appreciation of educational software.

The teachers' role

An aspect that relates to the issues of organization concerns that of the teachers' own perceptions of their role in facilitating the learning operation. The use to which a computer is put in any one classroom will hinge on how much the teacher views and accepts a role of facilitator or director of learning. The *director* will want a tight control on the flow of the learning operation; the *facilitator* may be happier in a more open-ended environment. Both will look for appropriate software to complement their styles; part of the challenge that educational software has to face is the dichotomy between producing material that will be considered acceptable compared with material that may lead into new territory. A fear that the computer may replace the teacher has resulted in the idea of putting the more tedious aspects of any subject onto a program in order to release the teacher for more worthwhile tasks. This must be the most charitable explanation for the vast number of drill and practice exercises currently produced, the sole aim of which is to test content. Conversely the imaginative use may appear to threaten the very foundations of the teacher's role and justification of existence. It is a case of the initiator versus the intermediary. The four paradigms — instructional, revelatory, conjectural and emancipatory — that Kemmis et al. (1977) described as useful in relation to placing computer-assisted learning in the field of education, can be seen as relevant here.

The *instructional* depends upon the subject content being readily broken up into small parts. Each part can be treated independently, and so there is the opportunity for reinforcement at each stage for the learner. Indeed it may be the most obvious mode for a machine that is associated with accuracy within a testing environment. This application is manifested in programmed learning units, or drill-and-practice exercises; such exercises on a computer offer the particular advantage of immediate feedback compared with the more traditional worksheet. But I would suggest this represents little advance.

The *revelatory* paradigm guides the student through a process of learning by discovery in which the content and related theory are revealed by progress through a unit. Hence the name, which reflects the assumption of the gradual unveiling, during the learning operation, of the key concepts. The use of simulations on computers is considered a classic example of this paradigm and is undoubtedly a method of capitalizing on the computer's particular assets.

The *conjectural* paradigm covers that area where the student learns through his experience at experimentation and exploration of any topic. Thus the computer may assist in the student's articulation and testing of his own ideas and hypotheses. This suggests an environment for modelling whereby the student himself has the opportunity not only to examine, but also to change, the internal working of a model.

The *emancipatory* paradigm hinges upon the concept of the computer reducing the amount of inauthentic labour of the learner, thus releasing him for the more significant work which is an integral part of his learning. This mode covers the facility of the computer to handle large quantities of data, or large tedious calculations. In this way, it may often appear in parallel with other paradigms.

These paradigms provide a useful framework within which one can examine the position of appropriate software. The emphasis that emerges from this framework is one whereby the style of learning operation that is fostered is a key. It is for this reason that I consider the software itself to be the determining factor.

The determining factor — software

The discipline base

Indubitably the key to the current use as well as future potential of the micro lies in the software which may be used. Taken in its broadest spectrum, I take this to include use of a programming language for the purposes of enhancing the nature of selected aspects of a discipline or information processing and as a mechanism for further study. A recent paper by mathematicians places significant emphasis on this aspect (Fletcher, Johnson, Lusty et al. 1983). For the purposes of this chapter however I intend to confine myself to those aspects of software which are attractive to the Humanities. Despite the concern that we may not yet have reached 'a critical mass' of software, certain strands are relevant at this stage.

The teacher coming new to the medium must have available material which can display the variety of the possibilities now open to him. Here we immediately face a problem — software that is designed to enhance existing teaching practice and current discipline content will be most immediately attractive to teachers. If it can be seen to be relevant to their current concerns and provides a coherent and attractive resource, there is a chance that the teacher will be prepared to try it out, to experiment and even shift some of their existing methods to accommodate the package. This will be the case in particular where software is seen to offer an opportunity to cover an aspect currently difficult or impractical by other means.

Unfortunately, if all software is designed to enhance existing material, then it is in reality being prepared for yesterday's classrooms. The ever-changing curriculum must take software along with it; software must be firmly aligned with the innovative movements within any one discipline (Watson 1982). It is often in this field that there can be enormous potential for a shift of relationship between the micro and a curriculum. Rather than the former serving the latter, we may now plan a shift whereby the curriculum itself takes into account the role of the micro within it, in the same way that a science curriculum and the laboratory are firmly intertwined. There will be important ideas, such as information processing and retrieval, which, through the availability of this medium, may become more significant concepts in their own discipline. This will be referred to later in the appropriate section.

Indeed, there is a clear case for considering the role of the micro not just within an individual discipline's concerns of content and concept, but across a whole range of related disciplines. The existing curriculum framework using a discipline structure can be an inhibitor to innovative thinking. Within the Humanities we can see broad sweeps of overlap, in the history/geography/economics area, and also the links of language/literature and communication in English and foreign languages. Yet the move towards integrated studies in Secondary schools is on the wane. So despite the overlap of interests, the first test any software will have to undergo is whether it fits into the current subject-based curriculum.

Despite this structure, certain key strands can be traced, and I intend to relate the actual examples below not only to the last three educational paradigms of Kemmis, but to aspects of content versus concept, and overall pedagogic methodology. Thus the thesis of this section depends upon the assumption that in educational software such strands should be drawn together.

'What would happen if . . . ?'

There can be no doubt that the advantage of computer simulations is now well established (Rushby 1979; Rushby 1981; Maddison 1982; Masterton and McCormick 1982; Nash and Ball 1983). The facility to simulate reality in a way which may not be feasible in the classroom received much attention in the mid-seventies, and most appropriately within the aegis of the science curriculum. Thus experiments that were difficult, dangerous, time-consuming or costly need no longer be left out of the school curriculum. Pupils are given the opportunity to explore a known environment, whether it is a pond over a period of years, or a nuclear reactor. They may examine the situation dynamically rather than statically by the opportunity to change the variables involved. The interactive potential, i.e. the facility for the pupil to respond dynamically during the program sequence, may be seen in its classic form here — pupils are engaged upon discovery learning through the opportunity to ask the question, 'What would happen if?' (Lewis and Want 1979).

It would be a mistake however to leave simulations within a scientific environment alone. Other disciplines such as geography and economics encourage their pupils to embark upon discovery-learning exercises through the use of simulations. Thus one piece of software, PUDDLE, encourages the geography pupil to examine the flow of water dynamically through a block of land, and watch the water that arrives as rainfall moves from vegetation and ground surface, through the soil and into the ground water. The opportunity to change variables, e.g. the season, the type of rainfall, the duration of the rain, enables the pupil to examine the impact upon the levels and rates of such interrelated through-flow and base-flow. It is impossible to examine this happening in the field and yet an understanding of the dynamic interrelationships is essential if the pupil is to gain an insight into the effect of moving water on the landscape. Economists use simulations as a method of considering the interplay of variables when managing a variety of scenarios from the BRITISH ECONOMY (Herriott Watt 1982) to a small factory (WORKER 1983). Kemmis et al. (op. cit.) consider this method part of the revelatory paradigm.

Model examination

Related to simulations must be the whole aspect of model examinations and appreciation. What is a model? Why do we use one in education? How can we determine a theoretical model? How 'accurate' need such models be to be educationally valid? All these questions may be posed by pupils, who themselves were quite happy to use models of real life in their normal play when younger. But the concept of modelling reality is more difficult within an academic environment and pupils often find it difficult to accept their nature and the opportunity to explore them. Thus programs which enable the pupil to understand the nature of models by exploring the interplay of variables which are integral to them, are attractive particularly to the economists. A simulation of a pond depends upon the use of an exact set of variables which reflect the interplay of conditions within the pond, e.g. herbivores, phytoplankton and fish. In this case, the model used is static and controlled by the user. The examination of a model for running the British economy (FISCAL) has no such known factors to be taken into account. The variables are a reflection of the interplay of the forces that a theorist has used to construct a model. Thus model examination by use of software is a way of facilitating an understanding of the transitory nature of the actual 'model' and its role within the learning and operational understanding of economics. Indeed the historians are also interested in the role of modelling as a methodology for relating a potential structural appreciation of events and the interplay of related forces. Blow (1983) has made a clear case for using a computer model to reinforce an understanding of 'real' history as opposed to simply making generalized statements about the past.

Rushby places model building and examination in the *conjectural* role, although it would seem that the form of model building and examination that is becoming apparent particularly within economics and geography straddles both the *conjectural* and *emancipatory* modes.

Hypothesis testing

The opportunities created by software for the student to test out a hypothesis when examining a model should be evident. Historians use hypothesis testing as a methodology within their own discipline, yet using a very different base. A historical understanding comes from the ability to understand the nature of historical evidence and to test hypotheses against such evidence. Thus we have here not a model as a basis for a simulation, but a core of evidence that needs to be sifted to identify various possible strands. The textual nature of such evidence may be daunting in computer terms, but it need not be presented in this way. What is difficult for the pupil to understand is that the facts do not necessarily speak for themselves, nor are they an indicator of the motivation and directions of the key characters at the time. Testing the evidence involves an ability to sort and rank its significance in the light of one's hypothesis. One such program (AMWEST) presents the pupils with a combination of eight factors which could have affected the growth of towns in the American West. They are given the task of identifying the four most significant factors and then ranking them in order of importance and interrelationship. They can therefore work in response to a hypothesis — e.g. 'The presence of a fort was essential to the growth of a town'. Thus the organization aspects of a computer come into play in a conjectural mode, at the service of the historian, and other disciplines who use such techniques.

'What shall I do?'

Decision-making itself can be encouraged by the style and nature of the simulation that is presented to the pupil. Work in the Humanities suggests that an increasing amount of CAL is encouraging the pupils not to change combinations of variables as a method of exploration through an environment, but to choose for themselves the most appropriate paths given a variety of options. 'Thus the cornerstone of the purpose has shifted from an analysis of the model by changing the parameters, to an analysis of the users' response in a variety of scenarios' (Watson 1983, p.147).

This is often exemplified in particular within a gaming framework where the pupils are encouraged to adopt roles. This has been used to effect in history, geography and economics. All have the unifying strand of placing the pupil in the role of a player within an environment, whether Edward I at Crecy, a sailing ship's captain, or a manufacturer of supermarket trolleys (Watson 1984a). The attraction of role-playing in this context is the facility for total involvement in the learning operation; the seeking out of information upon which a decision can be based places the content of the subject firmly within a conceptual framework. The opportunity presented by the computer is for the pupil to see speedily the results of his actions; such speed also provides an environment for the pupil to explore, to try out various paths even though not sure of the most appropriate route.

The program WINDS places the pupil in the position of a sailing ship's captain; there is no alternative source of power and the pupil, having chosen the ports between which to sail, has to respond to the wind directions that are given. No one can bail the pupil out — the decision that is taken will determine the boat's path. An exercise designed to foster an appreciation of the different wind zones of the world, it places the learning operation totally in the hands of the pupil. One key question that is raised is whether there is an appropriate transfer of learning from the response to winds on the ocean and how those same winds affect the climate of the surrounding continent. It would seem possible that this aspect of decision-making, by forcing the pupil to be so actively involved, may be powerful.

Games

It is too easy to equate computers with video games and to be concerned with the apparently drug-like qualities of such games as Snapper or Rocket Raider.

These really should not be used as an excuse to dismiss games as an educational methodology, which after all has been well accepted for some time (Taylor and Walford 1972). The subjects of English and geography have used games with some success. The opportunity for pupils to examine an environment from the viewpoint of a team-member, who has to work with other members of a team and respond to the alternative strategies of other teams given the same environment, can be enormously revelatory. Such games do not always work within an environment of winning and losing, particularly if the goals are various and can be determined by the players. Thus one team may prefer to opt for a safe steady life-style; others may be bold but risk the consequences of over-reaching themselves. Other games are not necessarily competitive; they are simply a framework within which pupils may adopt certain roles and follow through the likely actions and resultant consequences of their roles. The computer, as a manager of such games, acts as an emancipator in this form of learning, not only by handling tedious calculations or complex record sheets of progress, but by being a neutral presenter of the framework within which the roles are identified.

The game DEFCIT asks the pupils to form two teams; both have the same goal — to act as the Chancellor of the Exchequer to balance the budget, which is currently running at a deficit. The pupils have the use of three particular tools — revaluation/devaluation of the pound, inflation or deflation, and imposing/removing import tariffs. The teams may work one turn at a time *or* choose to operate the maximum five years at one turn. The flexibility of the team operation allows the pupils to work not in competition but in exploration of their role, and their own chosen way to operate the factors to reach a goal, and yet at the same time to compare their performance against others. In this case they will often opt for 'winning' by creating a large surplus, which in turn has ramifications on the budget in later years; thus they are forced to examine the real nature of the goal of balance during the game.

Group dynamics

Work in America on the appropriate scenario for computer use in education has often centred on the 'single student working at the computer' mode. Yarms (1982) reported that the aim at Dartmouth, USA, is to provide every student with individual on-line facilities both in the libraries and departments, and even in their dormitories. Some of these aims may be related to aspects of Tertiary education; is it a mode that would seem necessarily advisable, even if feasible, as the principle strategy within a Secondary school?

Following on the aspects of decision-making discussed in the last section, there is a natural extension of the question 'What shall I do?' into 'What would you do?', 'No, let's try it this way', 'Why not?' — that is, a discussion among a group of participants who may be seated around a keyboard working together as a group.

Two strands of interest emerge from such discussions. The first is that for the style and design of the software to stimulate such discussion presupposes that there is no easily discernible path through the material; there may be a variety of possible paths, and the investigation may even be open-ended enough for there to be no fixed ending or goal. This is important if the micro is to be accepted properly in its role as a facilitator for investigative learning and thought. It is doubly important for a machine which is thought of as an exact accuracy-testing tool to be seen as appropriate by teachers of disciplines in which accuracy and content is not their first priority. It is this facility to generate open-ended investigations which will attract the Humanities teachers, such as historians, where the issues debated may never have a clear and definite route for learning.

A second strand that emerges from group discussion is that the pupils are not only 'talking geography' or 'talking history' — they may also be learning how to communicate their ideas among themselves, to formulate arguments and logical paths of thought through the demands of group decision-making. Such debates take place around the neutral keyboard, which places the onus on the pupils for their response. The teacher is able to withdraw or intercede in the debate in a more valuable way than that of 'directing' the learning. Such a strengthening of communication is a direct aim of the English teacher.

A program, TRAY, has been developed to actively encourage the discussion of the possible content of a passage which initially appears as a complete blank — it could be prose or a poem. Letters or whole words can initially be guessed; as soon as a pattern develops, more care is taken and the discussion centres on the emerging shape of the passage and the hints the language gives. Pupils can send messages to themselves at various stages in the operation, which they can review at the end. This provides a powerful method of tracing their thoughts of both meaning and style as they work through the passage. Other questions posed to them may force their thoughts into certain directions. Trials among teachers and in classrooms have generated an amazing amount of discussion around the keyboard. Such a program could be considered emancipatory as well as revelatory.

McDonald (1977) further states that much of the learning that can be generated by CAL takes place away from the keyboard itself. Here is a powerful resource indeed if it can provide enough stimulus and motivation to extend the learning period. Videos of CAL in operation in some classrooms (CIC 1982; Institute of Education 1982) illustrate some of the intriguing aspects of group discussions generated by appropriate software.

The interactive classroom

Much discussion in the literature has taken place on the issue of the interactive nature of software, referring to the dynamic learning relationship between the pupils and software, as the pupils respond to questions and explore simulations. It would seem that for the Secondary school one wants to concentrate not just on the interactive dialogue between user and software, but on the interaction within groups or even the whole classroom. Figure 7.1 attempts to illustrate the various strands that might draw together interlocking sets of actions where there is a micro in the classroom. Such fluidity can encompass a range of uses from the electronic blackboard to the single learner at the keyboard, with a range of styles of software from the instructional to the emancipatory. It suggests that the learning environment can be such as to extract the maximum benefit of the micro if the software that is available is categorized in terms other than just that of a discipline content.

The database

The fact that large quantities of data can be stored on a computer is in itself of little interest. Large quantities of data are already stored all over the world in various libraries and filing cabinets. It is the ready access plus facility to interrogate such data that makes computer databases of such interest to educators. Historians in particular have been quick to grasp the nettle, and their current concern with encouraging pupils to examine historical sources places such data as census returns, parish records and trade directories in a fascinating position. The key to successful use is in the pupils understanding the nature of the data and thus asking appropriate questions. I see, for example, the role of a specific purpose package, CENSUS ANALYSIS, as a facilitator for the pupils to formulate their enquiry around the actual historical nature of the material. How many children in 1851 were working

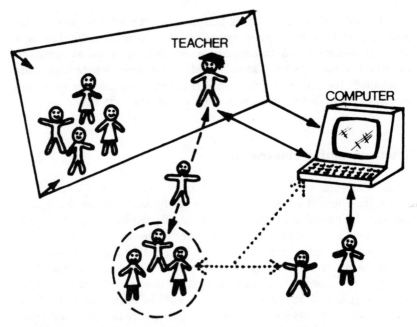

Figure 7.1 Single, group and class sets — the interactive classroom

before the age of sixteen? What sorts of job? What types of household still had children at home at sixteen? Is there a difference between girls and boys?

Some general purpose data interrogation packages such as MICROQUERY and MICROLEEP may offer a structure which enables historical, but also geographical, or administrative questions to be asked. It is important that the nature of the enquiry determines the outcomes rather than the structure of the software. In some Tertiary work, a particular set of statistical routines, Statistics Package for Social Sciences (SPSS), available on a large number of mainframe computers, appears to have had an unwelcome influence upon the style of research questions being posed. General purpose data packages are only useful when they can accommodate rather than constrain the nature of the data and enquiry.

The chance to ask appropriate questions, to be followed up by secondary searches, so fining down the nature of the enquiry, is valuable not just within a content base. The concept of searching paths that break up the structure into various component parts is fairly significant; routines that enable the pupil to appreciate the nature of such structures through defining the interrogation path must be of value in their overall understanding of the nature of data structures. There are many circumstances in which one wants the pupil to appreciate such a concept well beyond the confines of a school-based discipline. In fact in some ways that may be considered a particular contribution towards the aims of an awareness of information technology (Fothergill, op. cit.).

Word processing

In order to take full advantage of the role that word processing can have in the Secondary school, it is necessary to postulate an environment whereby every pupil has ready access to a micro with both a word processing facility and printer at school and for homework. Only then can the potential be realized. In the meantime much discussion can take place over the value of using such a facility to learn to draft material, re-order thoughts, try out alternative words and phrases, correct, insert and reorganize the words into the passage that is required. Research in Edinburgh (Pain 1981) has indicated that this facility, when made available to a group of poor learners and school refusers, had a significant motivational effect on learning. The positive asset of self-correction, rather than responding to a series of red ink, is powerful. The ability to overcome poor manual dexterity through the use of the keyboard is obviously significant. Are we yet in a position to anticipate a time when such word processing facilities are available? Should we remember the rapid advent of the electronic calculator in the hands of the pupils? Were the keyboard to become available to all pupils (as inevitably it must; at issue is merely the question of time-span), then interesting questions are posed about the nature of handwriting as a primary skill.

In the immediate term, the drafting and editing facilities of a word processor may be of more relevance to the English teachers when looked at in the context of creative writing. Rather than as a facility to draft and write accurate reports, it becomes a medium for the examination of the structure of a piece of writing. The ability to jumble words at random, and to examine patterns and images that emerge in text, places the word processor beyond just the role of a skill facilitator. It can be used for appreciation of literary structure — not the arid adverb counts in famous texts, but as a method of analysing the cadences and framework of texts by sorting techniques. Additional facilities such as a thesaurus and dictionary which are already common on many office word processors would enable such a device to be used in its full role — not just emancipatory, but revelatory and conjectural. Thus the conceptual aspects of English and its communicative framework seem more powerful than the content or skill-specific aspects of word processing.

The curriculum response

Evidence of current practice

It is, needless to say, extraordinarily difficult to attempt any overview of what is currently happening with micros in schools, just as it is difficult to say with any certainty what is happening in any domain. There can be little doubt that there has been a phenomenal growth in computer studies; does this account for all the time when micros are being used? Some case studies such as the MEP series (Chandler 1983; Watson 1984b) would suggest that in some schools there is already interesting activity along the lines that I have indicated as possible in the previous section. Undoubtedly it is piecemeal.

It would be false however at this relatively early stage to suggest that educational computing in Secondary school is a damp squib that has failed to ignite. Much work has to be done to overcome the variety of barriers before the average history or English teacher is aware of the potential and has the tools at his disposal to put it into practice. Nevertheless the thrust of the last section has been to suggest that the tools in terms of appropriate software are increasingly becoming available. These tools can be traced through in two parallel strands. In the first place there is always a discipline content, whether geography, history, French or English. But running in tandem are other strands such as encouragement to make decisions, the use of role-playing as a motivator, and opening up of access to appropriate data by the learner's manipulation of the material, the development of communication.

It is true that the educational world is littered with the fruits of curriculum development studies that, thoroughly lauded in the educational world, have never got over the barrier of poor dissemination or an appropriate framework for take-up. One such framework is that created by the examination system. Whatever the outcomes of the current deliberations over 16+ may be, it was reported at one examination board's meeting in March 1983 that there did not seem to be any need for the examination bodies to take note of the advent of micros in schools. The boards, after all, were in the main coping with testing a core of content; the professionals seemed to be explaining that the micro was simply another tool which teachers would use to teach that core of content. Thus the emancipatory potential in conceptual understanding is neither noted nor responded to. The pressures on the Secondary school teacher, locked into an examination system which makes enormous content demands, are such that any innovation has to be treated with considerable caution especially in the 14–16 age range.

The Information Technology school

Unlike other shifts in education, however, the advent of educational computing comes with a force of other interested parties behind it. There will be micros in schools in increasing numbers; indeed they seem to breed rather rapidly, and particularly when they are taken up by departments other than Computer Studies. There is a pressure of interest from the pupils, the home and society to know what the computer is being used for. It is of course possible to imagine the worst scenario whereby the computer is taken out of the cupboard occasionally, dusted off and used for drill-and-practice exercise to check spelling of the names of capitals of countries. Another scenario, by Hoyle (1983), suggests that the shift of emphasis which will come from use of good CAL is caught in the Catch 22 of innovation. I have an innate optimism in that core of energetic and imaginative teachers who will take others along with them.

The school's resource base often operates from diverse locations, audio-visual aids in one section and spread across departments, books within the domain of the central library as well as departments, external resources such as the local archive office possibly five miles away. Physical concerns of access inhibit their efficient use; sometimes departments consciously or otherwise duplicate some resources to facilitate access. Do we know the total resource base in our school? What index system can we use to interrogate the resource base?

The power of the computer in this area is enormous. It should be totally feasible, through networking, to interrrogate a central resource index from any one department as to particular data and their location. The important aspect is not that all the resources need to be centrally located, such as in a huge circular room with islands feeding off it in the classic sense of a resource base. The key lies in the information flow about the resource and its appropriate location. As long as the information is gathered, encoded and regularly updated then the user can search the data from a distance in the same way as Ceefax or Oracle enable users to search teledata in their own home. Data stored in this way need not be the equivalent of only library catalogues — they can encompass synopses of the data entry, and of course software itself can be pulled down. Thus let us imagine a pupil who wants to find out all information stored in the school in whatever medium on earthquakes. From the micro in the geography classroom they can explore the contents of the geography department library, the central library, the list of slides or film-strip sequences, the location of worksheets, and, particularly, if there is an appropriate piece of software which the pupil could use. In the future, the school's computing facilities will be able to down-load other information which may be relevant from sources well outside their physical school base.

This in turn will put an alternative perspective on the concept of distanced learning. I believe the main thrusts of the effect of computers will be not to de-institutionalize the process of education, and assume it will take place increasingly via home-based computers, but to provide a facility for any one institution to call upon various strands of data that are relevant that distance has in the past inhibited. The distanced-learning techniques, as applied for instance by the Open University, will now be applicable for operation *within* rather than *beyond* the institution. This in turn places another perspective upon the role of the computer as a facilitator for learning.

A revolution

Anyone looking at current practice in Secondary schools in late 1983 would be naive to suggest that a revolution is under way. But we have come a long way since 1979 in that the facilities are becoming available whereby a revolution may occur. The field is ripe for a major shift of educational thinking and methodology in the light of the advent of micros. This shift needs to be in the hands of educators; as Walton (1983) has indicated there are chances that in a fast-changing society adaptation may take place by default, and a technological elite will determine the change, to the detriment of educators. There is every evidence that society is grappling with the position. An Alvey Committee has been set up in response to the Alvey Report (DOI 1982), which itself had the brief to look at the nation's response to the impact of fifth-generation computers.

The Secondary school environment will take part in such a shift of emphasis when it can see the educational applications in a positive, rather than threatening way. I would suggest that computers may be able to facilitate the adoption of some key concerns, in terms of principles and styles of learning to be fostered, in a way that other constraints have hitherto prevented. Perhaps there is a need for a report similar to that of the Bullock Report (DES 1975), that could stress the need for whole schools' policies for educational computing as Bullock did for language. To a certain extent, the Microelectronics Education Programme, funded by the DES, attempts to have a similar influence. The current initiatives of the MEP are relying on an in-service pattern of a recursive nature (Rushby et al. 1981) in order to foster an overall awareness of the computer, its operation and potential in the school.

In the last decade there has been an increasing emphasis on the study of the 'Curriculum in Action' (Galton and Moon 1983). This has highlighted the intricate and diffuse web, composed of curriculum development and research projects, LEA influences, HMI influences, the school and the individual teachers, which cause the curriculum to stay on the move. We will see this curriculum respond to educational computing when we see the last mesh of the web, the teachers taking up the challenge that the software presents to them.

Most educational software is developed by national projects which actively involve teachers in the design and development stage. Thus ITMA (Initial Teaching Using Micros as an Aid), Netherhall School, Five Ways School, AUCBE (Hertfordshire Advisory Unit for Computer Based Education), the ILEA Educational Computing Centre, and CIC (Computers in the Curriculum Project), all produce computer-assisted learning material that other teachers would feel confident to use.

The interest taken by subject associations is another heartening indicator. The Geography Association has had a working party on educational computing for the last four years; the Economics Association for the last two. The Historical Association has called a one-day conference in February 1984. The National Association for the Teachers of English set up a commission to look at computers in English teaching in 1983. The foreign language community has begun similar initiatives. The Schools Council took the initiative to set up and support the Computers in the Curriculum Project as early as 1973; this project continues to work ten years later in the field of sciences and the Humanities, and has recently developed strong links with other curriculum development movements, e.g. The Economics Association 14–16 Project, the Schools Council History 13–16 Project, Schools Council Geography 16–19 Project, the Institute of European Education's Graded

Test Scheme, and the Association of Science Education's Secondary Curriculum Review.

Thus the concern of society is there; active involvement of teachers in development is there; concern of the subject associations is there. The current software gives clear indicators that the computer can be used in a way that takes us beyond it being an alternative teaching resource. The potential for the learner, and for a shift in the environment in which learning may be fostered, tutored and exploited is ready; the question surely is not whether this potential will be explored, but over what time period.

Summary and conclusions

Educational computing in the Secondary school faces the problems that are peculiar to it in terms of the Secondary environment. Despite this, software on the micro can be developed that follows two strands — that which is related to the content and concepts of a particular discipline, and that which is related to broad pedagogic aims. The former is a required and a necessary stage in the development process so that the fullest pedagogic potential can then be realised. Unlike many other forces for curriculum change, the issue of the micro in the school is already receiving significant attention from government agencies, the subject associations and the teachers themselves. It would seem logical that the curriculum in action will soon reflect the key influence that computers can have through use of appropriate CAL material on the development of the pupils' thought processes and the structures within which they learn.

CHAPTER 8

CONTRASTING APPROACHES TO THE LEARNING PROCESSES IN SPECIAL SCHOOLS

EVELYN CHAKERA

'But learning involves more than facts — it involves the learning of techniques, processes or skills'.

(Howe 1975, pp.297–8)

The interpretation of the learning processes quoted above cannot be applied to much of the teaching that has traditionally been practised in schools for children with severe learning difficulties. The approach often adopted has involved the implementation of behaviourist techniques; the child's learning is defined in terms of behavioural objectives. The curriculum is divided into main core areas; each core area is divided into components; each component is then broken down into targets; and each target is then analysed in terms of all the steps that compose that target. A child is taught each step systematically and does not proceed to the next step until the preceding one has been mastered according to pre-specified criteria. The steps are defined in terms of behavioural objectives — 'The child will be able to . . .' — which often state not only the actual behaviour required but also the setting, the number of 'correct' trials required, the time allowed for each trial etc.

The basic belief underlying this approach is that children with learning difficulties cannot and do not learn in the way that 'normal' children do. For this reason they need a very structured learning environment in order to help them acquire the skills that they will need in life. There have been many books published which explain the philosophy of this approach and, in some cases, include details of whole curriculum areas defined in terms of objectives. Examples of this type of approach include: Brennan (1979), Foxton and McBrien (1981) and Rectory Paddock School (1982).

A behaviourist approach is contrasted by a cognitive approach. The latter regards learning as the acquisition of information which is then represented in complex mental structures. These mental structures are composed of concepts with increasing levels of abstraction. Initially, learning occurs through direct activity which is then internalized. This is followed by the use of mental images to represent reality and later by the use of symbols. The development of symbolic representation enables one to develop complex and abstract concepts. Information must be gathered in such a way that it can be organized into the mental structures that form one's knowledge of the world. Linkages are made between items of information gained, which lead to more complex mental structures.

The congnitive approach has its roots in the theories of Piaget, Bruner and Vygotsky. Bruner (Bruner et al. 1965) and Vygotsky (1962) have both studied the role of the individual in the process of concept formation. The abililty to think and use concepts aids the understanding of experiences and the role of the learner in the acquisition of concepts is an active one.

Piaget (1972) has described how a child develops from being capable of certain logical reasoning processes only with concrete objects or events in the immediate present (the concrete-operational 'stage') to the formal-operational 'stage' where he can reason hypothetically. He explains the development of the understanding of concepts as a changing process. Initially, active participation in one's environment is essential in the form of exploration, manipulation and interaction. It is only later that one can reason in terms of verbally stated hypotheses and without the actual physical activity. The quality of the learning will depend on the nature of the activity and how it is linked to the child's present level of learning. J.McV. Hunt describes this as the 'Problem of the Match' (Whitehead 1976, pp.61–63). He suggests that learning occurs when one's present level of competence is matched to a new experience in such a way that it is neither too familiar and therefore uninteresting not too complex and therefore frustrating.

This is of course an over-simplified description of the nature of the learning process. There are many other models of learning besides the two outlined above, and the descriptions are themselves simplified. But this has been done in order to illustrate the contrast between them, and it is the dichotomy of these two approaches which has led to contrasting uses of microcomputers in learning.

The contrasting roles of the learner and of the microcomputer within these two approaches

A behaviourist approach assigns the child to a passive role in the learning process. Although the objectives are stated in terms of what the child will be able to do at the end of the learning experience, the content and method of the learning have already been specified by an adult. With a cognitive approach the child has a very active part to play in his learning. Although the teacher has to organize the child's learning environment in such a way that learning can occur (see Piaget and McV. Hunt above) it is the child's activity which determines the learning outcome. The activity leads to understanding, which in turn leads to the ability to use the knowledge acquired. Without understanding a child may be able to describe a concept (in symbolic form) but will not be able to employ it. It is therefore useless to the child in terms of increasing his understanding of the world.

These contrasting approaches have led to different exploitations of computers in Special schools. When they were first introduced into education in the 1960s, computers were used very much as sophisticated teaching machines. Their role was to present programmed instruction in the way outlined by Skinner — a behaviourist approach to learning. The computer was seen as valuable because of its properties of infinite patience, uniformity of presentation to each student, consistency of reaction, immediate feedback and reinforcement, and assurance that nothing was omitted from the piece of instruction or illogically presented.

Many drill-and-practice type programs were produced in the 1960s and still are today. Packages and kits are available for almost every area of the curriculum. The computer can be programmed to present each of the steps that comprise a target in such a way that the child is not presented with the next step until the prerequisite criteria for the present step have been met. The child is presented with a piece of information, tested on it and, if he responds correctly, he is then presented with the next item.

The computer is seen as more of an information resource than a teaching machine by exponents of a cognitive approach to learning. A computer has the capacity to simulate processes and can be used to help the child learn not only a fact but also the 'how' and 'why' of that fact. Howe and his colleagues (1979 a and b) at the Department of Artificial Intelligence at Edinburgh University have looked at the structure of knowledge and the teaching processes, techniques and skills which make use of the knowledge. They emphasize the importance of interaction between the learner and his environment in the formation of new models within a system which give rise to ever more complex representations. Learning occurs through interaction and therefore activity on the part of the learner. Howe does, however, believe that some structure is needed in the learning processes and that the teacher's role is to supply this structure. Without structure the learning would be haphazard.

Papert has taken the learner-centred view of the learning situation to extreme lengths. In the introduction to his book, *Mindstorms* (1980), he describes the knowledge and skills that children acquire spontaneously and without any deliberate formal instruction, and contrasts this with the difficulty and often failure that they encounter in the structured learning situation. He maintains that children learn by doing and thinking about what they are doing and they should therefore be the ones who are in control of the learning situation. Papert sees computers in education as tools to be used by the children to test out ideas and discover concepts, rather than being used by teachers to teach these things.

Different learning styles

The exponents of rigid techniques based on behavioural objectives and Papert, with the total freedom that he offers to the child, illustrate two contrasting interpretations of the way that children should learn. Studies by Pask and Scott (1972) and Bruner (Bruner et al. 1965) have shown that different people adopt different strategies in a given situation. In some exploratory research Pask and Scott (op. cit.) conducted experiments through which they hoped to find the optimum level of challenge and difficulty in a training programme so that students would retain their motivation. During the course of their investigations, Pask and Scott identified two main strategies employed by people when presented with a task. They found that some people tended to work through a problem, building up each concept sequentially, while others tended to jump from one idea to another and form a network of linkages into a final concept. They called the first group Serialists and the second Holists. Much classroom teaching tends to be Serialist in nature, as were the original programming materials. Although one can only make tentative generalizations from this exploratory and limited research, Pask and Scott concluded that a Holist could learn with a Serialist approach but that a Serialist could not cope with a Holist approach. Papert's approach to learning is more Holist in nature.

Bruner et al. (1965) looked at the ways in which one thinks about concepts. He described how, as an individual decides whether a given object is an example of a concept or not, he uses one of two strategies: Focussing or Scanning. Focussing involves using an initial example as a focus for subsequent examples, thereby checking each attribute in turn. Scanning involves eliminating concepts until one is left with the relevant one. In a situation where one has to learn something from material that is being presented, Bruner discovered that some people adopt what he called a Wholist approach where all the attributes of the first example are taken as an initial hypothesis; only elements that are common in subsequent examples are used to alter the hypothesis. Other people adopt a Partist approach in which only a part of the initial example is used to form the initial hypothesis and subsequent examples are used to decide whether to retain this hypothesis or formulate a new one. These different approaches lead to different ways of learning. A Focusser/Wholist will tend to learn one thing at a time and work in a steady logical progression towards a solution. A Scanner/Partist may have several things 'on the go' and achieve his solution through a gradual merging of ideas. The former reflects Pask's and Scott's Serialists and the latter their Holists.

Thus the work of Pask and Scott, as well as Bruner, has shown that some people have a definite preferred approach to learning. They may have considerable difficulty with a task that is presented in a conflicting way. Many people, of course, can cope with a variety of approaches and may even alter their strategy in different situations. Yet those investigations draw attention to the different learning styles which need to be considered when introducing new methods into the classroom.

Papert's approach to learning

Papert has used the programming language LOGO (see Chapter 5) to allow children to discover for themselves the principles involved in a particular concept and therefore to be in the position of understanding and not merely accepting a situation.

The Floor Turtle — a dome-shaped robot on wheels which is linked to a microcomputer — can be programmed using LOGO to move any distance and to turn in any direction one chooses and is seen by Papert as a means by which a child can see and experience certain concepts and ideas. Using LOGO a child is free to try out and test an idea. By experimenting with lengths and angles a child can discover for himself the relationship between the properties of shapes and be in a position of actually experiencing the building up of the relationships. The learner is in control of the Turtle's moves and, Papert claims, does not have the fear of making a mistake and being 'wrong'. Unlike instructional computer programs, the Turtle does not issue any evaluative comments on the program it executes. The child can see for himself the results of his program from the trail that the pen which is attached to the Turtle leaves on the paper. Papert maintains that if the child's program does not result in what he expected then it is not that the child has made a mistake but that the program has a 'bug' which can be found and eliminated. The principle is not that the program did not work because of something that the child did that was wrong, but that it could not work because of the 'bug'. In this sense, Papert does not mean bugs that are the result of trivial mistakes such as typing errors but those such as unsatisfied prerequisites, unprotected conditions, and conflicting prerequisites.

The programs first used in schools were instructional. Many of the kits and packages now being produced are too. Embedded in the programs were the content of the learning, the teaching style, the teacher's personality and correction methods. In the 1970s simulations followed the instructional programs and these could either be highly structured or very free. The teaching and learning strategy could be removed from the situation but the programs still contained some aspects of the curriculum. Papert claims that with the Turtle any prespecified curriculum is removed from the situation too.

There are instances when one has to accept facts without explanations or without the chance to work it out for oneself. This could include situations when one does not need to understand the fact to use it or where one does not have the capabilities to understand the fact at that time. It could also be that the amount of time it would take to discover the fact for oneself would be disproportionate to the value of the learning outcome of that process in some situations. Furthermore, after having experimented with a Turtle and made it move to one's commands, there comes a time when one wants to have a problem to solve. It is possible to think of a problem and then set about solving it but a learner needs something to guide his pursuits. Traditionally the teacher has structured the learning situation, posing problems according to a plan of development designed by the teacher. Papert argues that there should be no external structure because the pupil's investigations themselves would suggest the next step to him and, because he is thinking about what he is doing, the next step would be the natural development of the thought process.

Many pupils are used to the situation where the teacher is in control and might well have difficulty adopting the approach advocated by Papert. Many would want guidelines as to what to try next and many teachers would argue that without external advice one cannot guarantee that thought processes would develop naturally and logically as Papert claims.

For children with severe learning difficulties it would seem even more unlikely that learning would occur in the way that Papert describes. Not only do they have limited mental abilities, these children have problems and difficulties which can include poor concentration, lack of initiative, reliance on others for answers and dependence on externally organized instruction in the learning situation. These factors, which affect the learning of children with severe learning difficulties, are not only internal to the child but also external products of the learning situation itself.

As stated earlier, many of the learning situations that children with severe learning difficulties will have encountered will have been carefully organized into small steps so that predefined skills are built up 'properly'. Because it can take these children so much longer to learn a particular skill, it is felt that they must be helped to acquire it through a succession of small successful steps so that it is more likely to be retained correctly and therefore used correctly. The possibility of making a mistake or of giving up is reduced because each step is carefully matched to the child's present level of knowledge. However, this approach does not allow the child to think for himself and encourages reliance on external agencies. It can also lead to the development of isolated skills with the child unaware of the final goals and of the interlocking nature of knowledge. Skills can be very rigid when they are trained skills.

In order to evaluate the possibility of using the approach advocated by Papert with children with severe learning difficulties, a Turtle and a 'BIGTRAK' were taken into a Special school in Birmingham. A BIGTRAK, as was explained in Chapters 3 and 6, is a programmable toy tank brought out by Milton Bradley Limited in 1981. It is battery operated and can be made to move and turn like the Turtle, but it is not connected to a microcomputer. It does not have a pen attached and leaves no permanent record of its path. By pressing the appropriate keys one can program up to 16 commands at a time which BIGTRAK will then execute. BIGTRAK is controlled by the operator and does not issue any evaluative comments on one's program. It can therefore be used in a similar way to the Turtle to implement many of Papert's principles.

The investigation

This investigation was carried out in order to assess the extent to which computerized devices such as Turtle and BIGTRAK could be valuable as aids in the education of young people with severe learning difficulties. It was not the possibility of using these devices as additional media for the presentation of organized instruction that was being considered — this has been shown elsewhere (see, for example, Maxwell 1982 and Wharry and Thorne 1982) — but the extent to which they might be used by the youngsters as learning devices in the way that Papert envisages.

The group chosen for the investigation comprised five 16 to 19 year olds. These five satisfied the criteria that: they would be able to read the symbols on the keyboards; they had some understanding of number; and they could express themselves well enough to be able to indicate movements. All five boys had attended the same Special school for most of their school careers and were in the same class group. None of them had previously used either a BIGTRAK or a Turtle and they had had little experience of learning in the way that is envisaged with these devices. They had all had a little experience of using a computer in the context of a behaviourist approach to the learning situation. This had taken place a year previously when a computer and some drill-and-practice type programs had been loaned to the school for six weeks.

The boys therefore all had a similar educational background but they differed from each other in the following ways:

Boy 1 was confident if he was initiating a situation or if it was familiar. If he was at all unsure he would not act or answer but wait to be told, or watch to see what someone else did first. He could count up to 20 and indicate which of two numbers in this range was bigger or smaller fairly consistently. He understood the idea of moving forward and backward physically and of turning but was not very sure of left and right. He had no physical disabilities or sensory losses. He was able to understand spoken language involving the use of tenses, and hypotheses such as 'What . . . if . . . ?'. His expressive language tended to be restricted to one- or two-word answers to questions, but he used longer phrases if he was initiating the conversation.

Boy 2 was the most able of the group. He would try to answer questions when they were put to him and did not look to the others for a lead. He could add and subtract numbers up to 20 using counters and could indicate which number was bigger or smaller or which number came before or after another with numbers up to 99. He understood forward, backward, left and right to the extent that he was able to move or turn as requested. He had no physical disabilities or sensory losses. He was able to understand language at a similar level to that of Boy 1, but his expressive language was better. He expressed himself more freely and used a variety of questions, statements and interjections in a conversation.

Boy 3 liked to be sure of what he had been asked before answering or acting and would frequently check. He could count mechanically up to about 60 but was not confident about the relation of different numbers above 20. He too understood forward and backward, but hesitated over left and right. This boy also had no physical disabilities or sensory losses. His receptive and expressive language were similar to those of Boy 2.

Boy 4 tended to answer or act without stopping to think. He could follow an idea if he had initiated it, but tended to 'switch off' if the situation became at all demanding. He could count mechanically up to about 20 but found it difficult to indicate which number was bigger or smaller or name the next number without counting through to it. He was not very certain of directional terms. He had no physical disabilities or sensory losses. His receptive language was at a similar level to that of Boys 2 and 3. His expressive language was more like that of Boy 1, but with a little less reserve.

Boy 5 liked to be the centre of attraction and would turn the situation to his way if he could. He had the least understanding of number of this group. He could count up to 10 but did not understand the numbers and would guess or say something completely unconnected to divert attention from the point in question. He could indicate forward and backward, but muddled left and right. He too had no physical disabilities or sensory losses. His receptive and expressive language were more limited than those of the other four. His understanding of tenses was not always correct and he found it difficult to hypothesize. His expressive language consisted mainly of words or phrases designed to make the others giggle.

The boys were shown how to make the BIGTRAK move by pressing an arrow key, then a number key and then 'go'. The other functions were not introduced. After watching a few moves the boys were invited to try for themselves. Left to themselves, none of the group could make the BIGTRAK move at all and none of them was prepared to keep trying until he succeeded. They all needed to be talked through the steps several times before they could actually make it move through their own endeavours.

The results of these endeavours were analysed with reference to the four strategies that have been identified by Eisenstadt and Kareev (1977). These are strategies that can be employed when faced with a problem involving the scanning of a situation in order to perceive the position displayed. One extracts information about a situation by examining the external representation of it which is physically there in front of one, but one has to be able to have internal representations which one can apply to the scanning process. Eisenstadt and Kareev describe their four strategies as:

(1) Confirmatory — one already has a hypothesis in mind when approaching a situation and employs a strategy to confirm or refute it.
(2) Exploratory — one does not have any hypothesis when approaching a situation but intends to discover something from the situation.
(3) Revival — one is sure of a particular situation and uses the encounter to confirm it.
(4) Imaginary — one looks at the situation and imagines the outcome of a particular action.

Any of these four strategies can be applied when faced with the problem of commanding a BIGTRAK or Turtle to move along a particular path or to a particular point. One can program the moves and watch the machine to check that it does actually follow the proposed path. This would be a Confirmatory approach. One can type in a series of commands in order to see which movements result from them — thus using an Exploratory approach. If one is sure that a particular command will elicit a particular response then a Revival approach would involve using a series of known command-action instructions to control the movements of the BIGTRAK or Turtle. And an Imaginary approach would involve the pre-planning of a movement or set of movements before they were actually executed.

One needs to learn the appropriate approach to employ when faced with a problem-solving situation. In order to control the movements of the BIGTRAK or Turtle it is necessary to be able to develop the ability to scan the situation and have a definite strategy with which one can hope to execute a plan of action. If one only wants to make the machine move and is not concerned about the exact nature of the movement, then it is less important to have a definite strategy. In this case one simply has to learn how to program the commands, without wanting or needing to link this to an intended movement or to the outcome.

However, the implementation of a particular sequence of movements, whether through necessity or design, in order to achieve a particular objective requires the implementation of a strategy. The group of young people involved in this investigation showed the implementation of all four of the strategies in different circumstances, but the Revival approach was the most common (see Table 8.1). This was with the BIGTRAK.

Table 8.1 Strategies employed by the five boys when using the BIGTRAK

Strategy	Number of boys using this strategy spontaneously	Number of boys using this strategy with teacher intervention
Confirmatory	1	4
Exploratory	1	5
Revival	5	5
Imaginary	2*	3*

$n = 5$, * in a limited way

Three of the boys (3, 4 and 5) became confident of the procedure required to make the BIGTRAK move forwards. They restricted themselves to this movement. They could not, however, estimate how many lengths were involved if they were trying to make it reach a particular point and they stated their aim in terms of the direction and not the goal. All three limited their experiences to learned procedures of which they were certain. One of the boys (2) was confident about the backward movement and was prepared to use this in a Revival approach: if the BIGTRAK was in such a position that it could only move backwards, he would use this movement; if it could move either way, he chose the forward movement. Only one of the group (1) was prepared to use all four directional arrows and he did this using an Exploratory approach. He was not able to understand the two turning operations but he did know that by pressing either of the two arrows '◄—' or '—►' the BIGTRAK would rotate. None of the group was able to use an Imaginary approach except in a limited way, with the forward movement. Two of the group (1 and 2) could make a guess as to where the BIGTRAK would stop if ' ♦ 10' or ' ♦ 2' were pressed but only with this gross distinction. They could not imagine intermediate movements with any real accuracy.

Each of the four approaches was introduced to the group through teacher interaction in order to ascertain whether or not the boys would use them. The Confirmatory approach was tested by asking the boys where they wanted the BIGTRAK to go and how they would execute this movement. Four of the boys (1, 2, 3 and 5) could select the appropriate arrows after each arrow and the corresponding direction in the room had been discussed. They then used a Confirmatory approach since they were not certain enough to be able to employ a Revival approach.

The introduction of the Exploratory approach highlighted two of the problems the boys were having when faced with the decision as to which arrow to select. They were very interested in the results of the programming but had two difficulties. One was in expressing verbally the movements of the BIGTRAK. They could indicate that it had moved 'That way' by pointing, but could not use the terms 'forwards', 'backwards' etc. The second difficulty involved their short-term memory ability; they could not remember the program that they had employed to execute the move that they had just watched. The boys thus found it difficult to discover what a particular set of instructions would do. This meant that they could only employ an Imaginary approach in the limited way described above. With teacher interaction, three of the boys (1, 2 and 3) could state whether the BIGTRAK would move forward or backward if either of the two appropriate arrows was selected, but they were unable to imagine anything more involved than this. The problems encountered by the boys can be related to Vygotsky's theory that a child can learn the symbolic form from adults, in this case the arrows representing directions, without having a greater understanding of the symbols. They were also finding it difficult to appreciate the *value* of the numbers, although the number-names themselves were very familiar. These factors illustrate the argument that one can appear to know something but, unless one understands it, one cannot use it very successfully.

The Revival approach was restricted to forward movements in three cases (3, 4 and 5) and backward movements in two (1 and 2) but with limitations in the length of move. All of the boys knew which number they were selecting but could not link the choice of number with the distance that the BIGTRAK would travel. In all five cases the boys preferred to use the Revival approach. The possible reasons for and implications of this in the teaching and learning situation will be discussed in the summary of the results and the conclusions (see pages 157–160).

The Turtle proved to be more complex than the BIGTRAK. Firstly, the direction in which it was facing was not as obvious to the boys as it had been with the BIGTRAK. Secondly, they did not have the arrows to help them decide which way they wanted the Turtle to move. This meant that they had to name the direction, then select the key with the same initial letter as the direction chosen. One might have expected that it would be easier to name a direction and then select the appropriate key in this way, but it was harder for the boys to link this to the actual direction of movement than it had been with the pointing arrows on the BIGTRAK. The main difficulty was in the choice of number, since numbers which they could use in arithmetical operations, that is numbers up to about 20, did not cause much movement in the Turtle. It required numbers in the hundreds to move an appreciable distance and the boys did not have the concept of these.

The trail left by the Turtle allowed the boys to make comparisons, but only to the extent that they could see who had made it travel the furthest. They could not remember nor understand the numbers required to alter the previous distance to a chosen amount. Additional problems were caused by the actual format and positioning of the keyboard. If the boys touched more than one key at a time, or if the press itself was not precise, then the command was spoilt and they had to start again. Also, the keyboard was attached to the computer so that if they did not turn quickly after pressing the last key, the Turtle had executed the move before they had a chance to watch it.

All these problems, some of which could be overcome by making adaptations to the keyboard and to the Turtle itself, resulted in a greater dependence on the teacher. After instruction but without teacher direction, two of the boys (2 and 3) managed to use a Revival approach to make the Turtle move forward, each time using a distance that they had first been shown and that they knew would work.

All other attempts to make the Turtle move required some teacher intervention; either to help them work out the direction or distance or to rectify errors in the actual typing of the commands. So, in this form the Turtle proved to have a great number of limitations for this group. However, as Howe (1980) has illustrated, adaptations are possible and the Turtle could then probably be used by these young people in the way that Papert describes.

Discussion of the results of this investigation

As we have seen, Papert (1980), Maxwell (1982), Wharry and Thorne (1982) and others have described the value of the Turtle and BIGTRAK as tools which allow children to discover for themselves the outcome of their actions and to build up ideas from their direct experiences. And Beryl Maxwell has developed this point at some length in Chapter 5 of this book. Furthermore — 'Allowing a child to explore a LOGO system by exploring his or her own ideas and being rewarded by feelings of creative and aesthetic achievement uses the most powerful motivating forces' (Culwin 1983, p.64).

The results of the investigation outlined in this chapter prompt the question, 'Does this description apply to youngsters with severe learning difficulties?'. All of the boys seemed content to use those commands of which they were certain. None of them showed any signs of experimenting or of considering, 'I wonder what would happen if . . . '. Of course it is not possible to conclude that they did not think along these lines; it is only possible to state that none of them expressed this or acted in this way, except, to a degree, the one boy (1) who explored the four arrow keys on the BIGTRAK. The boys all appeared to enjoy their experiences with the Turtle and the BIGTRAK and asked to have another turn at a later date. Only boy 4 did not show a lot of interest in the devices. The most noticeable outcome of the experiment was the extent to which boy 1, who was normally very reluctant to do something unless he was absolutely certain, was prepared to use the Exploratory approach to this situation. Further experiences with these or similar devices would perhaps increase this confidence and lead to its extension into other areas. Further experiences might have led to the development of reactions in these boys similar to those described by Culwin (op. cit.), but the problems caused by using the devices without modification did not warrant additional experimentation at this stage.

The fact that they limited themselves to known procedures highlights one of the main differences between the young people involved in this investigation and those in the studies described by the other authors in the earlier chapters of this book. The boys in this study lacked the ability to discriminate and generalize and were limited to employing techniques of which they were certain. This could in part be the result of the nature of their education. If their teaching has followed a task-analysis approach, the boys will have acquired particular skills in particular ways and then had to learn to generalize those skills. If they have not been given sufficient opportunity to generalize the skills, they will be limited in their capabilities to learn from situations. These young people tended to wait to be told what to do with the Bigtrak and the Turtle rather than trying to learn for themselves. The introduction of computerized learning techniques as embodied in the Bigtrak and Turtle could help these young people to acquire the skills needed for generalization to appropriate contexts, that is, to learn from their experiences.

Making a mistake is an important step in the learning process. If a particular action does not result in the expected outcome and one has therefore made an error in implementing a plan or in calculating the outcome, or has failed to take account of circumstantial factors, one learns not only that 'A' does not lead to 'B' but also that 'A' does lead to 'C'. One learns that 'C' is not 'B' and that 'C' is related to 'A'. Winston (1977) expounds the value of this situation in his article on conceptual thinking. He explains that in order to develop a concept one must, as would be expected, have examples with which to identify that concept, but equally important are examples which do not form part of that concept. Non-exemplars which are close to the concept enable one to define the limits of the concept in question. To be of value, a concept must have boundaries so that one can use it; experience of examples outside the boundaries helps to define those boundaries. In a similar way, results of 'A' that lead to 'C' define the limits of 'B' and thus enable one to draw conclusions about the outcomes of the situation 'A'.

With Turtle and Bigtrak, by experimenting with the commands in the way that Papert advocates, a child can build up concepts by discovering their boundaries. Any 'mistake' that he makes will help him to define the limits of the boundaries. Papert takes the position that traditional teaching methods fail to help children to learn the whole of a concept. With youngsters with learning difficulties this problem is even more acute. Because of their limited mental abilities there is a danger that they will only be taught what they 'need' to know and not be given the chance to learn the concept in context. A child could be taught to program the Turtle or BIGTRAK to make quite complex movements. This could be achieved by carefully building up a number of known commands and moves until the child can execute the complete set himself. However, the youngster may be unable to judge the results if, for example, one distance is altered by one unit. If he has not been given the chance to experiment with the distances and turns, then he will not be in a position of knowing, or at least being fairly confident, that though he alters a particular dimension by a particular amount the device will finish in roughly the same place, or, that by combining two different moves the device will finish in the same place. By being allowed to experiment the child will be able to learn the range of movements that lead to a particular goal and those that do not, rather than being restricted to the one route that he has been taught.

The ideas described above give some idea of how the computerized learning principles of the Bigtrak and the Turtle can help the child to learn rather than be taught. The Bigtrak and Turtle themselves are perhaps too complex as an introduction to learner-centred computerized learning techniques for youngsters with severe learning difficulties; but the principles that underlie their use in the classroom could be employed.

Two of Howe's colleagues have designed a button box to replace the keyboard as a means of entering the commands into the computer in order to control a Turtle (Emanuel and Weir 1976). They replaced the complexity of keys on the keyboard with just 12 buttons. This meant that a child could locate the button that he wanted more easily, and without being faced with redundant possibilities. This would greatly simplify the task for a youngster with learning difficulties. Emanuel and Weir also designed the buttons so that they lit up and remained alight until the command had been executed by the Turtle. If the button could remain alight until the child was ready to start the next command, it would enable him to compare the chosen button and the resulting movement more readily. He would not need to remember which button he had pressed. This would give him two concrete clues as to future possible moves. The button box could be numbered in such a way that a large range of distance could be covered with just a few numbers. For example, the number five could be equivalent to pressing 999 — the maximum for the Turtle — on the conventional keyboard.

Thus if the child understands the numbers one to five, and knows how each relates to the others, he is only required to use numbers with which he can actually operate. As well as reducing the number of buttons, it would be necessary to alter the spacing of those of the Turtle and the BIGTRAK too. Many youngsters with learning difficulties have poor motor control and often miss the key they were intending to press or touch two keys at the same time. If each key or button were well separated from the next, then this would not happen. For some youngsters, controls using parts of the body other than the hands might also be needed.

It is very difficult to distinguish the front and the back of the Turtle and therefore to decide whether it has to move forwards or backwards. The addition of some features, for example a face, would make this clearer. The boys in this investigation had to stand by the Turtle or the BIGTRAK and face the corresponding way in order to decide the direction of a chosen goal. The arrows on the BIGTRAK helped them to recognize the direction, but a combination of arrows and directional words — forward, backward, left and right — would help the development of their understanding of direction. A portable keyboard/button box could be an intermediate step between moving *oneself* in the way one wants the device to move and *imagining* the move.

These young people did not have the ability to be able to experiment with the keys until they could work out the function of each. Both the Turtle and the BIGTRAK have far too many keys for this. However, if a simplified keyboard was used, the number of keys could be reduced to the maximum that any one particular child could cope with. Even a board with only one function key could be given to a child. With no instructions or suggestions he would have the chance to discover and learn for himself what to do. In this way more controls can be introduced gradually without altering the learning to a task-analysis approach. A task-analysis approach of the conventional kind would deviate from the learning principles that underlie the use of these devices.

Summary and conclusions

Youngsters with severe learning difficulties need to learn to be more independent of the teacher in the learning situation. They need to be given the opportunity to try out ideas for themselves and to develop the ability to learn from what they do. They need to develop the confidence to try out a hypothesis and cope with unexpected results.

At present there is very little in the way of software available for youngsters with severe learning difficulties. The preparation of each program can take many hours and many teachers are opposed to the introduction of computers into the classroom. 'Containment of an innovation is a well-polished talent of the educational system' (Goodyear and Barnard 1982, p.67).

Papert, too, describes the socio-political forces which work against innovation in the classroom (Papert 1980). Many regard the use of computers with youngsters with learning difficulties as a leap by Special schools onto the current bandwagon. But perhaps, if the emphasis were placed on the development of devices which employ the learning principles of BIGTRAK and Turtle, in a simpler form, then the value of these computerized learning principles would be recognized.

For youngsters with learning difficulties it will always be necessary to have intervention on the part of the teacher in the learning situation. Learning as envisaged by Papert would not be possible, not only because of the limitations of time, but also because of limitations in the youngster's mental capabilities. They need to be helped to acquire as many thinking skills as possible from their educational experiences. Devices such as BIGTRAK and Turtle could be used to teach them those skills which the more widely used approaches fail to do.

CHAPTER 9

IN CONCLUSION

VIC KELLY

For those readers who may have worked diligently through this book, it seems not right to leave things now in the air. Some attempt must be made to pick out the main strands running through the individual chapters and to draw the main threads together. To do this it might have been sufficient to suggest that readers now return to the Introduction, and perhaps also to Chapter 1, and reread these in the light of what has been said in the subsequent chapters. There is a real sense, however, in which what has been said in the intervening chapters requires and makes possible certain additions to, or certain modifications of, the points which were made there.

The Introduction began by making three points or posing three hypotheses. These were that there is great educational potential in the microcomputer, that this potential is not always being tapped in current uses and that at least part of the reason for this is the lack of teacher expertise and of appropriate help for teachers in acquiring this expertise. All three of these hypotheses have been confirmed by the accounts of the succeeding chapters. It is possible now, however, in the light of those accounts to elaborate a little further on these issues.

It has certainly emerged incidentally that a good deal of current use in schools is somewhat mundane and unimaginative. For it is clear that still the most common uses to which the microcomputer is being put by teachers are either the teaching of computer studies, with the associated concern with the learning of one or other of the computer languages, or the teaching of largely factual aspects of other subjects or of the so-called 'basic skills', with the concomitant concentration on 'drill and practice' exercises. Such uses may have their place in schools, but if this is the only use to which the micro is put, then we must as teachers look forward to the day when the micro will replace us, even those of us who teach computer studies, since this kind of use offers no role for the teacher as educator, and the mere teaching of subject-content can probably be achieved more effectively and more cheaply by beaming appropriate programs to children in their own homes. Distance learning is already with us, but we must not be fooled into thinking that distance education is to be so readily achieved. A micro would certainly be as effective as a Mr Gradgrind or a Mr M'Choakumchild in teaching those FACTS which for them constituted the sole and total concern of schooling — and, indeed, of life — but what Dickens was at pains to reveal through those characters was that there is a good deal more to education than that, and most teachers too, I believe, would wish to claim the same. If this is so, we must take the trouble to identify what this is and especially to explore what the micro may be able to offer us in our attempts to attain it. For it should not be allowed to go unnoticed that the major initiative behind the current development of microtechnology in schools has come from the Department of Industry rather than from the Department of Education and Science, with all that that implies in terms of its underlying theory or 'philosophy', and that this is only one of several recent initiatives from the same source. Thus, this process of deflecting our attention from education to instruction, from the Humanities to the Sciences, from the liberal to the vocational, from the worthwhile to the utilitarian, from intrinsic value to extrinsic purposes, has already begun. We mentioned in the Introduction that the advent of the microcomputer could lead to a revolution in education; we must take every step to ensure that this is not the kind of revolution that will lead to the overthrow of education itself.

We must consider very carefully, then, as was suggested earlier, what the potential of the microcomputer is for education in the fullest sense, and this is a question on which the accounts given in this book have thrown a great deal of light. It is one of the central purposes of this chapter to attempt to pick out some of the major features of this. We must attempt to end on a positive note, since the main purpose of this book has been to identify some of the real advantages offered by the microcomputer for the advancement of our educational goals.

Extending the teacher's powers

Perhaps the most important factor which emerges from the case studies we have offered is that the micro can offer incredible opportunities to the teacher who is prepared to see it, not as a gimmick, nor merely as an aspect of modern society which education must come to grips with, but as a tool to increase the range of his or her professional competence, to extend the scope of his or her powers as a teacher. We have seen, perhaps especially from David Dodds' chapter, the potential the micro has to enhance the ordinary project or topic work of the Primary school, to take its place alongside work in art and craft, in science, in environmental studies, in language, in mathematics and so on, and to add something both valuable and new, a dimension whose advantages are manifest and which could be provided in no other way. For there is no doubt that, in the projects he describes in Chapter 3, the children's understanding and appreciation of what they had observed had been enormously enhanced by the use they had been able to make of the powers of the microcomputer.

The use of the microcomputer as a database in an exercise such as that described by Alistair Ross in Chapter 4 is another good example of the possibilities which it offers for extending the teacher's powers. The processes of data collection, storage and retrieval clearly offer great potential for children's learning. For they enable them to take responsibility for their own learning, to feed to the machine their own data, to appreciate from this that the machine can do nothing except through their own control of it, to recognize the need for précis skills, for economy of language, for the coherent classification of data, and to learn to frame their own hypotheses and pose their own questions and to test their hypotheses and to find answers to these questions through a processing of their data of a far more sophisticated and complex kind than they or even their teachers can provide. Perhaps the most important thing they will learn in this way is that answers to questions cannot go beyond what is contained in the data provided, and if this does no more than encourage them to be properly sceptical of most of the knowledge they are offered, it will have done all that Socrates once tried to do, and, perhaps, a good deal more.

This is one example of how the microcomputer can be used to perform some of the donkey work, to take over some of the mundane chores that often stand between pupils and the essential elements in the learning processes their teachers are attempting to promote. But we have also seen how, at a simpler level, it can perform this kind of function for us, for example by taking the role of a highly sophisticated calculator to take the complex mathematical computations out of, say, work in Home Economics on dietary balance or work on many topics in science, especially in physics. Problems over mathematical calculations have often got in the way of learning in other subjects; the microcomputer offers us a device for eliminating this complicating factor, so that children can get more directly to grips with the essential concepts of the subject.

However, it is not merely in removing barriers to conceptual development that the microcomputer has a major part to play. The account of Beryl Maxwell in Chapter 5 of her work with LOGO in mathematics, along with that of Charles Bake in Chapter 6 of the work he has undertaken in mathematics with other kinds of program too, reveal some of the positive potential offered by the micro for assisting with the promotion of children's conceptual development, for helping them towards the acquisition of the kind of understanding which will increase their own powers of mind. For we have stressed that education is about learning to think rather than about coming to know, and, if this is so, then it is conceptual understanding rather than merely knowledge which is its main concern. These chapters, together with Evelyn Chakera's account in Chapter 8 of her experiment with severely retarded adolescents, reveal some of the ways in which learning of that kind can be supported by the proper use of the microcomputer and, what is perhaps more important, how the microcomputer can offer more effective support for this kind of learning than most other aids to which a teacher might turn.

We have stressed constantly that this kind of learning requires an active engagement on the part of the child, especially through opportunities for experimentation and 'learning by discovery'. It is perhaps in the scope it offers for such experimentation that the micro has most to offer. For there are many areas in which experimentation is not possible, perhaps because it might be dangerous, perhaps because it is impracticable. Programs offering simulations provide a useful form of substitute in areas of this kind. Direct, concrete, first-hand experimentation is clearly not possible in areas like those of concern for the geologist or the economist; certainly experimentation is not physically possible in these areas on the scale that would be necessary for any significant results to be obtained or for meaningful learning to occur. The kinds of simulation game and program described by Deryn Watson in Chapter 7, however, do provide opportunities for experimentation of this kind, for playing with the variables — of a nation's economy for example — to see what the results might be, or to frame hypotheses about the likely effects of one's actions or decisions and to test those hypotheses in simulation. This is another extension of the teacher's powers which the microcomputer offers and it requires little imagination to gauge its significance and its possibilities. It also makes it quite clear that we should not, as our Introduction might have suggested, condemn games and even preprepared programs out of hand; we must, however, evaluate them very carefully against well thought out educational criteria.

A further important point which follows on from this, and which also emerges from Deryn Watson's account of some of the possibilities of the microcomputer in teaching and learning in the area of the Humanities, is that we will be doing ourselves, our pupils and even the microcomputer a disservice if we see it as a tool that can be used only in situations where precision and accuracy are needed. For, if we take this view, we will return the machine again to the mathematics and/or science departments and ignore its potential in other areas. For again what has emerged from the accounts we have offered is the facility it offers 'to generate open-ended investigations' (see page 136) and it is this, far more than its precision and accuracy, which constitutes its main attraction and defines its main contribution to the process of education. It can be used by teachers and pupils alike to experiment, to try out ideas, to explore areas of knowledge where hard and fast answers are not only impossible but also undesirable. It is a major facilitator of those processes of enquiry, exploration, hypothesis-framing, hypothesis-testing, and general critical consideration and analysis of data, which constitute the essence of education.

These, then, are some of the ways in which, properly used, the microcomputer can offer the teacher an extension of his or her powers of a kind and on a scale that can be found nowhere else. Much depends, however, on the teacher's ability to take advantage of what is offered and this brings us to a second major issue that has emerged from our earlier chapters — the impact of the new technology on teachers who have not grown up, either personally or professionally, in the computer age.

The teacher's expertise

Several contributors have commented on the unwisdom of providing schools with the hardware of microtechnology without first providing the teachers with the expertise to make proper use of it. A number of points must now be made about this.

First of all, we might see this as a chicken/egg, cart/horse kind of problem. For, to be fair, one can imagine similar criticisms being levelled at authority if it had provided intensive courses for teachers in the use of microcomputers in the classroom before it had provided the microcomputers for them to use.

Secondly, we must note that a good deal of help has been and is being offered to teachers in this area. We mentioned in our Introduction that the Microcomputers in Education Project has had teacher education as a very high priority and many other agencies have set up courses of various kinds for teachers wishing to familiarize themselves with the new technology.

A more telling and justifiable criticism, however, may be that directed at the kinds of course teachers have been offered. The experience which Beryl Maxwell describes of attending such a course and being not only bewildered by the jargon and the technology, but also discouraged from pursuing it in her work by the absence of any indication of what its real educational potential might be, would, I imagine, be an experience that many teachers would admit to having shared, and the dissatisfaction she describes would be one that many teachers would echo. Too often these courses are offered by people whose expertise lies in computer programming and in the manipulation of the machines; too seldom is it matched by any kind of expertise, or even of appreciation, of the concerns of education and the ways in which the new technology might be harnessed to promote these concerns. We must be grateful that Beryl Maxwell met her Floor Turtle and fell in love with it. Not every teacher who has attended that kind of course has enjoyed the same fulfilling experience. Most have returned with more of that computer-induced anxiety, which Leslie Smith described at length in Chapter 2, than they had when they set out. It was for this reason that Leslie was asked to write that chapter; and, indeed, this was a major reason for publishing this book. For it was clear from the outset of this survey that a major barrier to the achievement of anything like the full potential of the microcomputer in education is the attitudes generated by the lack of teacher-expertise.

It is for this reason that this concluding chapter must stress two things, two lessons about teacher expertise which emerge from our earlier chapters.

The first of these is the simplicity of much that our contributors have described. Many of the uses to which they have put their microcomputers to great effect have not required massive and sophisticated expertise, have not involved understanding of jargon or of any complex computer language, and have not necessitated elaborate programming techniques. David Dodds made it possible for his pupils to feed in most of their information verbatim. Alistair Ross required his pupils to organize their data for the machine only as part of the learning process he had planned. Beryl Maxwell's pupils were able to say, 'LOGO is a very good computer language because it does not all have to be learned, because it is made up of the English language', 'This language includes the easiest of words that are not difficult to remember when you are using the computer', 'I find the language we use with the turtle (LOGO) is much easier to understand' and 'It is easy to learn and does not confuse me'. Charles Bake and Evelyn Chakera also used LOGO's Floor Turtle and BIGTRAK too, which again can be programmed simply in a language related to English. Even the more complex programs which Deryn Watson describes as available for use in Secondary schools come in a ready form and require of teachers little more than the skill to load them into the machine. Teachers do not need, then, to become expert programmers or to acquire skill in handling elaborate computer languages to make good educational use of the microcomputer. The problem with many courses for teachers in this area is that they assume that this is what teachers need. Even where individualized programs must be written, teachers of resource have established links with local Secondary schools or institutions of Higher Education and arranged for their computer studies students to write these for them. The degree of expertise needed, then, is nothing like so great as many teachers imagine.

A second point about teacher expertise that has emerged from earlier chapters is that it still remains the case that the major kind of expertise the teacher needs is his or her expertise as an educator. For by far the most important role for the teacher is that of evaluator, or even censor, of software, and judge of the value of the tasks that are being assigned to the microcomputer in schools. Not to put too fine a point on it, a good deal of the software being pushed at schools and at teachers is plain rubbish and teachers need to recognize that it is their task to evaluate this in educational terms and not as technological experts. It requires no expertise in computer programming to recognize the educational aridity, and even banality, of much that is currently on the market. Teachers must have the confidence to make this kind of evaluation of what they are offered in this sphere. In our Introduction, we suggested that all software was to be regarded with great suspicion. We repeat that advice here. What we must now make clear is that some of it has a lot to recommend it, especially those programs which are designed to promote pupils' thinking, to invite speculation and experimentation, to enhance their intellectual development. It is the 'drill and practice' and the content-based programs we need to be especially wary of, those written on the assumption that education is about the acquisition of knowledge — even of a trivial kind — rather than the development of powers of critical thought.

Teachers should, therefore, take heart from what they can read in this book. The technological expertise they require to make use of the microcomputer is far less than they may have supposed and the educational expertise they need to evaluate the programs they are offered continues to be the prime consideration.

A curriculum revolution?

So, what price a curriculum revolution? From what has been said earlier it will be apparent that this could take one of two forms. For, on the one hand, content-based, 'drill and practice', teaching-machine uses of the microcomputer could attain the ascendant and replace the teacher as a more efficient device for purveying knowledge and filling empty heads with bodies of information. This may be a particularly serious possibility in Special Education where the influence of behaviourist psychology, allied to the difficulties experienced by the pupils, has for long led to limited kinds of ambition on the part of practitioners and teachers, and where the possibilities of the microcomputer are therefore most likely to be viewed in terms of low level cognitive performance. But the dangers of this in all sectors of education are there to see and an effort is needed if we are to resist them. For, as was pointed out earlier, the prominence of the Department of Industry in this initiative is ominous, and we can look for little educational guidance or direction, or even understanding, from that quarter.

On the other hand, enough has been said in earlier chapters to suggest that a different kind of revolution is possible. For there is no doubt that the microcomputer, in presenting teachers with opportunities to extend the scope of their practice, faces them also with some important questions about what they are doing and why they are doing it. It requires of them that they ask some searching questions about education and its role in society. For, until they face and answer these questions, they will not be clear about how the microcomputer can be absorbed into their practice and included in their armoury of devices for the destruction of the bastions of ignorance, how they can ensure that it will extend their opportunities to educate the next generation rather than replacing these, and education itself, with some inferior substitute.

If we see the micro merely as a device to support what we are already doing and we thus encourage the production of software to provide that support, then, as Deryn Watson pointed out (see page 130), we will be preparing material for yesterday's classrooms. For continuous curriculum change and development is an every-present reality and the role of the microcomputer must be viewed in that context. We must ask what the microcomputer can offer us as an aid to that continuous development, and the earlier chapters of this book suggest that, if we genuinely pose that question, there are some fascinating answers that we might come up with and that these are such that might well lead to a curriculum revolution.

It would be naive to suggest that such a revolution has already occurred or is even on the horizon. But the advent of the microcomputer, and especially the means by which it has been introduced into schools, may be seen as a major factor in placing education at the crossroads at which it now stands. Which direction it now takes remains to be determined, but a choice must be made if it is not to be pushed by default into the direction favoured by the utilitarian and vocationally oriented factions whose control of schooling is increasing daily. If such a choice is to be made on sound educational grounds, it must be made by the educators. It is for this reason that they must familiarize themselves, as a matter of some urgency, with the crucial issues which are at stake. It is as an attempt to contribute to that process that this book has been compiled.

BIBLIOGRAPHY

Allen, D. (editor) (1981) *Welcome to the BBC Computer Literacy Project.* London: British Broadcasting Corporation.

Armstrong, W.A. and Booth, C. (1972) The uses of information about occupation: Part 2 — an industrial classification, 1841–1891: Appendjx E — the occupations of 1861, 284–310 in Wrigley (editor), 1972.

Baker, K. (1983) Speech at Heinemanns Launch of Dudley programs, London: 19 September 1983.

Benjamin, H. (1939) The saber-tooth curriculum, in Hooper (editor), 1971, pp7–15.

Berger, P.L. and Luckmann T. (1971) *The Social Construction of Reality: A Treatise in the Sociology of Knowledge.* London: Penguin Books.

Blenkin, G.M. (1983) 'The Basic Skills', in Blenkin and Kelly (editors), 1983, pp29–56.

Blenkin, G.M. and Kelly, A.V. (1981) *The Primary Curriculum.* London: Harper and Row.

Blenkin, G.M. and Kelly, A.V. (editors) (1983) *The Primary Curriculum in Action.* London: Harper and Row.

Blow, F. (1983) *Computers, the Counterfactual and Causation.* Leeds, Trinity and All Saints College.

Blyth, A. (1976) *Curriculum Planning in History, Geography and Social Studies 8–13.* London: Collins.

Brennan, W.K. (1979) *Shaping the Education of Slow Learners.* London: Routledge and Kegan Paul.

Bruner, J.S. (1961) The art of discovery, *Harvard Educational Review* **31**.

Bruner, J.S., Goodnow, J.J. and Austin, G.A. (1965) *A Study of Thinking*. New York: Wiley.

Burton and Short (editors) (1983) *Sixth International Conference on CAL in the Humanities*. Maryland: Computer Services Press.

Callaghan, J. (1978) Speech at meeting of National Economic Development Council, December.

Chandler, D. (1983) *Exploring English with Microcomputers*. London: CET.

Coll, J. and Allen D. (editors) (1982) *The BBC Microcomputer User Guide*. London: British Broadcasting Corporation.

Computers in the Curriculum (1982), CAL in the Humanities (Video). London: Chelsea College.

Culwin, F. (1983) Turning Turtle, in *Your Computer*, 3, pp66–69.

Daines, D. (editor) (1983) *Micro Primer Reader*. London: CET.

Eisenstadt, M. and Kareev, Y. (1977) Perception in Game Playing: Internal Representation and Scanning of Board Positions, 548–564 in Johnson-Laird and Wason (editors), 1977.

Emanuel, R. and Weir, S. (1976) *Catalysing communication in an autistic child in a LOGO-like learning environment*. The Proceedings of Summer Conference on Artificial Intelligence and Simulation of Behaviour. Edinburgh: Edinburgh University Department of Artificial Intelligence.

Fletcher, T.J. (1983) *Microcomputers and Mathematics in Schools*: A discussion paper. London: Department of Education and Science.

Fletcher, T., Johnson, D., Lusty, T. et al. (1983) *The Microelectronics Education Programme and Mathematics*. London: Department of Education and Science.

Floyd, A. (editor) (1976) *Cognitive Styles*, Open University Course E201, Personality and Learning, Block 5. Milton Keynes: The Open University Press.

Floyd, A. (editor) (1981) *Developing Mathematical Thinking*. London: Addison-Wesley.

Fothergill, R. (1981) *The Microelectronics Education Programme — A Strategy*. London: Department of Education and Science Information Office.

Foxton, T. and McBrien, J.A. (1980) *Trainee Workbook*. Manchester: Manchester University Press.

Galton, M. and Moon, B. (editors) (1983) *Changing Schools . . . Changing Curriculum*. London: Harper and Row.

Garland, R. (editor) (1982) *Microcomputers and Children in the Primary School*. Sussex: Falmer Press.

Goodyear, P. and Barnard, A. (1982) Microcomputers and Special Education, Survey and Prospect, 61–73 in Smith (editor), 1982.

Govier, H. (1983) In defence of the 'Fakes', *Microscope* **9** pp11–12.

Gregory, F. (1983) An Approach to Teaching Information Handling, 46–61 in Daines (editor), 1983.

Holden, E. (1977) *The Country Diary of an Edwardian Lady*, London and Exeter: Joseph in association with Webb and Bower.

Holloway, M. (1982) A Role for the Microprocessor in Infant Education, 57–70 in Garland (editor), 1982.

Hooper, R. (1971a) Educational technology in the USA — a diagnosis of failure, 411–423 in Hooper (editor), 1971b.

Hooper, R. (editor) (1971b) *The Curriculum: Context, Design and Development.* Edinburgh: Oliver and Boyd in association with The Open University Press.

Hooper, R. and Toye, I. (editors) (1975) *Computer Assisted Learning in the United Kingdom: Some Case Studies.* London: CET.

Howe, J.A.M. (1975) Artificial Intelligence and Education, 295–317 in Hooper and Toye (editors), 1975.

Howe, J.A.M. (1979a) *Learning through Model Building.* Research Paper No.120 Edinburgh: Edinburgh University Department of Artificial Intelligence.

Howe, J.A.M. (1979b) *Some Roles for the Computer in Special Education.* Research Paper No.126. Edinburgh University Department of Artificial Intelligence.

Howe, J.A.M. (1980) Computers: A Researcher's View, *Special Education: Forward Trends* **7** (4) pp17–21.

Howe, J. and Ross, P. (1982) *Microcomputers in Secondary Education: Issues and Techniques.* London: Kogan Page.

Hoyle, E. (1983) Computers and Education: a solution in search of a problem?, 55–65 in Megarry, Walker, Nisbet and Hoyle (editors), 1983.

Hunt, J.M.V. (1976) Using intrinsic motivation to teach young children, *Educational Technology* **II** (2) pp78–80.

Inner London Education Authority (1980a) *People Around Us: Work.* ILEA Learning Materials Service. London: Inner London Education Authority.

Inner London Education Authority (1980b) *Social Studies in the Primary School.* ILEA Learning Materials Service. London: Inner London Education Authority.

Institute of Education (1982) Hertfordshire School Geography program (Video). London: Institute of Education (internal resource from Kent).

Johnson-Laird, P.N. and Wason, P.C. (editors) (1977) *Thinking: Readings in Cognitive Science*. Cambridge: Cambridge University Press.

Kemmis, S., Atkin, R. and Wright, E. (1977) *How do students learn? Working papers on Computer Assisted Learning*, Occasional Paper No.5. Centre for Applied Research in Education, University of East Anglia.

Lawton, D., Campbell, J. and Burkitt, V. (1971) *Social Studies 8–13*. Schools Council Working Paper No.39. London: Methuen Educational for the Schools Council.

Lewis, R. and Want, D., (1979) Educational Computing at Chelsea, 1969–79, 163–176 in Lewis and Tagg (editors), 1979.

Lewis, R. and Tagg, E.D. (editors) (1979) *Computer Assisted Learning — Scope, Progress and Limits*. Amsterdam: North Holland.

Lewis, R. and Tagg, E.D. (editors) (1981) *Computers in Education*. Amsterdam: North Holland.

Lewis, R. and Tagg, E.D. (editors) (1982) *Involving Micros in Education*. Amsterdam: North Holland.

Maddison, A. (1982) *Microcomputers in the Classroom*. London: Hodder and Stoughton.

Masterton, D. and McCormick, S. (1982) Some suggestions for CAL development in Science. CIC Project Paper 23. London: Chelsea College.

Maxwell, B. (1982) Meeting a Turtle, *Computers in Schools* **4** (3) pp10–11.

McDonald, B. (1977) The Educational Evaluation of NDPCAL, *British Journal of Educational Technology* **8** (3) p176.

Medawar, P. (1967a) Hypothesis and Imagination, 147–173 in Medawar, 1967b.

Medawar, P. (1967b) *The Art of the Soluble*. Harmondsworth: Penguin.

Medawar, P. (1972a) Lucky Jim, 270–278 in Medawar, 1972b.

Medawar, P. (1982b) *Pluto's Republic*. Oxford: Oxford·University Press.

Megarry, J., Walker D.R.F., Nisbet, S. and Hoyle, E. (editors) (1983) *Computers and Education*. London: Kogan Page.

Microcomputers in Education Project, Meeting of Northern Examination Boards, Leeds, March 1983.

Nash, A. and Ball, D. (1983) *An Introduction to Microcomputers in Teaching*. London: Hutchinson.

O'Grady, C. (1983) Growing doubts on micros scheme, *Times Educational Supplement* 17 June, 1983.

Open University (1982) *Micros in Schools*. Milton Keynes: Open University.

Pain, H. (1981) A Computer Aid for Spelling Error Classification in Remedial Teaching, 297–302 in Lewis and Tagg (editors), 1981.

Papert, S. (1980) *Mindstorms: Children, Computers and Powerful Ideas*. Brighton: Harvester.

Pask, G. and Scott, B.C.E. (1972) Learning Strategies and Individual Competence, *International Journal of Man-Machine Studies* **4**, pp 217–253, also Whitehead, 1976, pp 257–287, Floyd, 1976, 24–33.

Piaget, J. (1972) Intellectual Evolution from Adolescence to Adulthood, 158–165 in Johnson-Laird and Wason (editors), 1977.

Popper, K.R. (1959) *The Logic of Scientific Discovery* (revised 1968 and 1972) London: Hutchinson.

Rectory Paddock School (1982) *In Search of a Curriculum*. Sidcup: Robin Wren.

Rheingold, H. (1983) Video Games go to School, *Psychology Today* **17** (9) pp37–46.

Rogers, V. (1968) *Social Studies in English Education*. London: Heinemann.

Ross, A.G. (1982) Learning history with the help of a microcomputer, *Microscope* **6** pp10–14.

Ross, A.G. (1983a) Microcomputers and local history work in a primary school, *Teaching History* **35** pp10–14.

Ross, A.G. (1983b) The microcomputer in primary school social studies, *Social Science Teacher* **12** (3) pp82–85.

Ross, A.G. (1984) The strongest conker in the world: a scientific investigation by a primary class, to be published in *Microcomputers in action in the classroom*. Open University course P542. Milton Keynes: The Open University Press.

Royal Society of Arts (1982) Teachers Certificates of use of Computers in Education, Pilot Scheme. London: RSA Syllabus.

Rushby, N.J. (1979) *An Introduction to Educational Computing*. London: Croom Helm.

Rushby, N.J. (editor) (1981) *Selected Readings in Computer Based Learning*. London: Kogan Page.

Rushby, N., Anderson, J., Howe, A., Marrow, F. and Piper, D. (1981) A recursive approach to teacher training in the use of CBL, in Lewis and Tagg (editors), 1981.

Schools Council (1981) *The Practical Curriculum.* Methuen Educational for the Schools Council.

Shepherd, I., Cooper, Z. and Walker, D. (1980 *Computer Assisted Learning in Geography.* London: Council for Educational Technology with the Geographical Association.

Smith, C. (editor) (1982) *Microcomputers in Education.* Brighton: Ellis Horwood.

Stevens, A. (1982) School computers hinder learning, *Observer,* 24 October 1982.

Stonier, T. (1983) *The Wealth of Information.* London: Methuen.

Taylor, J. (1982) What makes good software? *Times Educational Supplement* 5 March 1982.

Taylor, J. and Walford, R. (1972) *Simulations in the Classroom.* Harmondsworth: Penguin.

Vygotsky, L.S. (1962) *Thought and Language.* Massachusetts: Massachusetts Institute of Technology.

Walton, D. (1983) Education and the New Technology, in Galton and Moon (editors), 1983 pp123–130.

Watson, D. (1982) Some Implications of Micros on Curriculum Development, in Lewis and Tagg (editors), 1982, pp197–203.

Watson, D. (1983) Humanities teachers write imaginative CAL, in Burton and Short (editors), 1983, pp732–753.

Watson, D. (1984a) The role of decision-making in CAL, *Computers and Education* 8.1, pp31–34.

Watson, D. (1984b) *Exploring Geography with Microcomputers.* London: CET.

Webster, F. and Robins, K. (1983) Listening to Money Talk, *Times Educational Supplement* 7 October 1983.

Wharry, D. and Thorne, M. (1982) Teaching with Robots, *Educational Computing* pp34–35.

Whitehead, A.N. (1932) *The Aims of Education.* London: Williams and Norgate.

Whitehead, J.M. (1976) *Motivation and Learning,* Open University Course E201, Personality and Learning, Block 3. Milton Keynes: The Open University Press.

Winston, P.H. (1977) Learning to identify toy block structures, in Johnson Laird and Wason (editors), 1977, pp199–211.

Wrigley, E.A. (editor) (1972) *Essays in the use of quantitative methods for the study of social data*. Cambridge: Cambridge University Press.

Yarms, W. (1982) a local network of personal and time-sharing computers, in Lewis and Tagg (editors), 1982, 19–23.

Government Reports and other official publications referred to in the text — listed in chronological order

Board of Education (1931) *Primary Education* (The Hadow Report on Primary Education). London: HMSO.

Central Advisory Council for Education (1967) *Children and their Primary Schools* (The Plowden Report). London: HMSO.

Department of Education and Science (1975) *A Language for Life* (The Bullock Report) London: HMSO.

Department of Education and Science (1978) *Primary Education in England: A Survey by HM Inspectors of Schools*. London: HMSO.

Department of Education and Science (1981) *The School Curriculum*. London: HMSO.

Department of Industry (1981) *Micros in School Scheme*. London: DOI Information Office.

Department of Education and Science (1982) *Mathematics Counts* (The Cockcroft Report). London: HMSO.

Department of Industry (1982) *A Programme for Advanced Information Technology* (The Alvey Report). London: HMSO.

Software List

AMWEST	Computers in the Curriculum, Chelsea College, London (under development).
ARROW	The Chiltern Advisory Unit, Endymion Road, Hatfield, Herts.
BIGTRAK	Milton Bradley Ltd.

BRITISH ECONOMY Edinburgh: Herriot Watt; Longmans Software.

CENSUS ANALYSIS Computers in the Curriculum, Chelsea College, London, Longmans Software.

CRASH Microcomputers in Education Project Software Packs (available from Tecmedia Ltd.)

DATAPROBE London: Addison-Wesley.

DEFCIT Computers in the Curriculum; Chelsea College, London (under development).

DLAN Campbell Systems, 15 Rous Road, Buckhurst Hill, Essex, IG 6BL.

EUREKA Microcomputers in Education Project Software Packs (available from Tecmedia Ltd.).

EUREKA ITMA, Longmans Software.

FACTFILE Cambridge Micro Software.

FISCAL Computers in the Economics Curriculum, Chelsea College, London, Longmans Software.

INFILE Leicester Education Authority.

LOGO CHALLENGE London: Addison-Wesley.

Micro-LEEP Inner London Educational Computing Centre, Bethwin Road, London, SE5.

MICROQUERY AUCBE, Hertfordshire.

Micro-SCAN Inner London Educational Computing Centre, Bethwin Road, London, SE5.

PUDDLE Computers in the Curriculum, Chelsea College, London, Longmans Software.

QUERY AUCBE, Hertfordshire.

RAYBOX I.T. Unit, Davidson Centre, Davidson Road, Croydon, Surrey, (under development).

RHINO Smile Centre, Middle Row School, Kensal Road, London, W10 5DB.

R.M.L. LOGO Oxford: Research Machines Ltd.

TAKE HALF Smile Centre, Middle Row School, Kensal Road, London, W10 5DB.

WINDS Computers in the Curriculum, Chelsea College, London, Longmans Software.

WORKER Computers in the Curriculum, Chelsea College, London (under development).

(Please note that software programmes are prepared for use with particular versions of hardware and may not always be compatible with machines approved for use in schools by the Department of Industry. Please note also that some require disk-drives, printers and other peripherals which may not be standard in many schools.)

Acknowledgements

The publishers gratefully acknowledge permission to quote from the following or for the use of illustrations.

page 39: CACE (1967) *Children in Their Primary Schools*, HMSO: p 188.

page 40: DES (1978) *Primary Education in England – a survey by HM Inspectors of Schools*, HMSO: p 50.

page 40: DES (1981) *The School Curriculum*, HMSO: pp 10–12.

pages 37 and 40: DES (1982) *Mathematics Counts*, HMSO: p 95.

All reproduced with the permission of the Controller of Her Majesty's Stationery Office.

pages 36, 59 & 60: Taylor, J. (1982) 'What Makes Good Software?' *Times Educational Supplement*, 5 March 1982, © Times Newspapers Limited.

page 37: Hooper, R. (1971) 'Educational Technology in the USA: a diagnosis of failure' in Hooper, R. (editor) *The Curriculum: context, design and education*, Oliver & Boyd/Open University Press (1971) © The Open University Press, 1971: pp 411–423.

page 41: Schools Council (1981) *The Practical Curriculum*, Schools Council: pp 18–19. Reproduced by permission from Schools Council Working Paper 70, *The Practical Curriculum*, Methuen Educational.

page 48: Digital Tracer, R D Laboratories Ltd.

page 49: Presfax Board, Schofield & Sims Ltd.

page 56: BIGTRAK, Milton Bradley Ltd.

page 57: Zeaker, Colne Robotics Company Ltd.

INDEX OF NAMES

Allen, D.,   30, 171, 172
Anderson, J.,   176
Armstrong, W.A.,   72, 171
Atkin, R.,   174
Austin, G.A.,   172

Bake, C.,   vi, xi, xvii, 107–124, 165, 168
Baker, K.,   126, 171
Ball, D.,   131, 174
Barnard, A.,   161, 173
Benjamin, H.,   1, 171
Berger, A.L.,   64, 171
Blenkin, G.M.,   14, 64, 114, 171
Blow, F.,   133, 171
Blyth, A.,   67, 171
Booth, C.,   72, 171
Brennan, W.K.,   145, 171
Bruner, J.S.,   66, 146, 148, 149, 172
Burkitt, V.,   174

Callaghan, J.,   126, 172
Campbell, J.,   174
Chakera, E.,   viii, xi, xviii, 145–161, 165, 168
Chandler, D.,   140, 172
Coll, J.,   30, 172
Cooper, Z.,   176
Culwin, F.,   157, 158, 172

Daines, D.,   172, 173
Dodds, D.,   vi, xi, xvi, 36–63, 107, 164, 167

Eisenstadt, M.,   153, 154, 172
Emanuel, R.,   159, 172

Fletcher, T.,   41, 42, 124, 130, 172
Floyd, A.,   172, 175
Forster, E.M.,   6, 18, 19
Fothergill, R.,   126, 139, 172
Foxton, T.,   145, 172

Galton, M.,   143, 172, 176
Garland, R.,   107, 172, 173
Goodnow, J.J.,   172
Goodyear, P.,   173
Govier, H.,   121, 173
Gregory, F.,   108, 110, 173

Hall, M.,   83
Holden, E.,   44, 173
Holloway, M.,   173
Hooper, R.,   37, 171, 173
Howe, A.,   176
Howe, J.A.M.,   125, 145, 147, 148, 157, 159, 173
Hoyle, E.,   141, 173, 174
Hunt, J. McV.,   146, 147, 173
Huxley, A.,   18

Johnson, D.,   130, 172
Johnson-Laird, P.N.,   172, 174, 175, 177

Kareev, Y.,   153, 154, 172
Kelly, A.V.,   v, viii, xi, xiii–xix, 1–19, 114, 162–170, 171
Kemmis, S.,   129, 131, 132, 174

Lawton, D.,   67, 174
Lewis, R.,   132, 174, 175, 176, 177
Luckman, T.,   64, 171

Lusty, T.,   130, 172

Maddison, A.,   127, 131, 174
Maiterton, D.,   131, 174
Marrow, F.,   176
Maxwell, B.,   vi, xii, xvii, 84–106, 152, 157, 165, 167, 174
McBrien, J.A.,   145, 172
McCormick, S.,   131, 174
McDonald, B.,   137, 174
Medawar, P.,   65, 66, 174
Megarry, J.,   173, 174
Moon, B.,   143, 172, 176

Nash, A.,   131, 174
Neaux, M.,   121
Nisbet, S.,   173, 174

O'Grady, C.,   62, 175
Orwell, G.,   18

Paiget, J.,   xiv, 52, 146, 147, 175
Pain, H.,   139, 175
Papert, S.,   xv, 12, 16, 55, 61, 63, 87, 148, 149–151, 157, 161, 175
Pask, G.,   148, 149, 175
Peters, R.S.,   14
Piper, D.,   176
Popper, K.R.,   65, 175

Rheingold, H.,   xiv, 175
Robins, K.,   125, 176
Rogers,   67, 175
Ross, A.G.,   vi, xii, xvi, 64–83, 164, 167, 175
Ross, P.,   125, 173
Rusby, N.J.,   125, 126, 131, 133, 143, 175, 176

Scott, N.J.,   148, 149, 175
Shepherd, I.,   127, 176
Skinner, B.F.,   61, 147
Smith, C.,   173, 176
Smith, F.,   6
Smith, L.A.,   v, xii, xvi, xvii, 16, 20–35, 113, 167
Steven, A.,   37, 176
Stonier, T.,   63, 176
Strong, T.,   114

Tagg, E.D.,   174, 175, 176, 177
Taylor, J.,   36, 38, 59, 60–61, 62, 135, 176
Thorne, M.,   55, 62, 152, 157, 176
Toye, I.,   173

Vygostky, L.S.,   146, 156, 176

Walford, R.,   135, 176
Walker, D.,   173, 174, 176
Walton, D.,   142, 176
Want, D.,   132, 174
Wason, P.C.,   172, 174, 175, 177
Watson, D.,   vii, xii, xvii, 125–144, 165, 166, 176
Webster, F.,   125, 176
Weir, S.,   159, 172
Wharry, D.,   152, 157, 176
Whitehead, A.N.,   9, 176
Whitehead, J.M.,   146, 175, 176
Winston, P.H.,   158, 177
Wright, E.,   174
Wrigley, E.A.,   171, 177

Yarms, W.,   135, 177

SUBJECT INDEX

Abbeydale Industrial Hamlet, 49–52, 63
Acorn, B., 30, 32
active learning, 9, 10, 11, 14–16, 146, 147, 148, 165
Advisory Unit for Computer Based Education (AUCBE), Hertfordshire, 83, 143, 178
algebra, 116
Alvey Report, The, 142, 177
AMWETT, 133, 177
Ancient History, 2
anxiety, 20, 35
ARROW, 96, 99, 177
art, 40, 41, 47, 164
arts, 19
Around Us, 66, 68, 173
Association for Science Education, 144
Association for the Teaching of Social Science, 64

BASIC, xiv, 84, 85, 86, 108, 110, 111
basic skills, xviii, 17, 40, 41, 60, 162
see also, skills
Beauchief Abbey, 49
behavioural approach to teaching, 147, 152
behavioural objectives, 145, 147, 148
behaviourist psychology, xviii, 5, 145, 169
behaviour modification, xviii
Bell, Andrew, 37
BIGTRAK, xvii, xviii, 55, 108, 116, 117–121, 151, 152, 153, 154–156, 157, 158, 159, 160, 161, 168, 177
Birdsearch, 45
Birdwatch, 4

Birmingham, 151
Board of Education, 39, 177
Brave New World, 18
British Broadcasting Corporation, 24, 30, 32
British Economy, 132, 178
Bullock Report, The, 143, 177

calculating, 17
calculation, 139, 164
Cardiff University, 55
Ceefax, 6, 50, 142
Census Analysis, 137, 178
Central Advisory Council for Education, 39, 177
coding, 71–73
cognition dissonance, 9
cognitive approach to learning, 146, 147
College of Education, 55
commerce, 8
computer advisors, 60, 107, 108
computer aided design, 61
computer games, xiv, 5, 6, 134–135 *see also*, video games
computer graphics, 22, 57, 106 *see also*, graphics
Computer in the Curriculum Project (CIC), xvii, 125, 137, 143, 177, 178
computer keyboards, 22, 25, 28, 30, 31, 32, 33, 86, 87, 117, 136, 139, 152, 157, 159, 160
computer languages, xiv, 5, 16–17, 54, 130, 149, 162, 167, 168
computer literacy, 2, 20, 21, 22, 23, 24–25, 26, 27, 31, 35, 61
computer program, 5, 6, 7, 10, 15, 16,

25, 30, 32, 37, 38, 43–44, 45, 53, 54, 59, 63, 85, 113, 114, 118, 120, 121, 129, 132, 147, 150, 161, 163, 165, 166, 169, 177–179

computer programing,   xiv, 15, 34, 36, 43, 45, 55, 57–59, 60, 61, 63, 86, 89, 106, 151, 154, 167, 168

computer science,   21

Computer Studies,   xiv, xvii, 4, 25–26, 27, 55, 66, 84, 125, 127, 128, 140, 141, 162, 163

concept development,   12, 40, 41, 43–44, 55, 66, 115, 141, 146, 147, 148, 149, 151, 158–159, 165 *see also,* intellectual development

control technology,   63

Country Diary of an Edwardian Lady, The,   44, 173

craft,   40, 164

CRASH,   xvii, 120, 121, 178

creative work,   39

creative writing,   139

critical awareness,   7, 16, 78, 166, 168

Croyden,   37, 114, 121, 123, 178

curriculum development,   xvi, 1, 23–25, 143, 169

curriculum planning,   4

database,   12, 45–46, 52, 53, 137–139, 164
   freeform,   46

DATAPROBE,   83, 178

data processing,   10–11, 13, 15, 52, 54, 64–83, 108, 130, 140, 141–142, 164, 166 *see also,* information processing

Dartmouth,   135

decision making,   134, 136, 140

DEFCIT,   135, 178

Department of Artificial Intelligence (Edinburgh University),   147, 173

Department of Education and Science,   xiii, 37, 38, 40, 41, 125, 143, 163, 177

Department of Industry,   xiii, 59, 62, 107, 114, 121, 126, 142, 163, 169, 177, 179

developmental psychology,   9, 146

Dickens, Charles,   163

digital plotter,   47

discovery,   39, 106, 129, 132, 165

disks,   34, 59, 68, 69, 79, 179

dissemination of innovation,   24, 140 *see also,* centre periphery model

DLAN,   57–58, 178

drill and practice,   xviii, 37, 61, 85, 107, 112, 113, 114, 115, 124, 141, 142, 147, 162, 168, 169

emotional development,   9

English,   125, 128, 131, 135, 136, 139, 140, 143

environment,   40, 41

environmental studies,   164

EUREKA,   112, 113, 127, 178

Europe,   22

examination,   140–141

experience,   9, 10, 11, 39, 40, 41, 85, 146, 157, 158

Eyam,   52, 59

FACTFILE,   108, 178

films,   7, 128

FISCAL,   133, 178

Five Ways School,   143

flashcards,   36, 112

food and dietary planning,   11, 165

foreign languages,   125, 131, 143

fractions,   112

French,   140

Further Education,   15

geography,   41, 47, 67, 125, 128, 131, 132, 133, 134, 135, 136, 138, 140, 142

geology,   165

geometry,   57, 116

Gibralter Point Nature Reserve,   44–48

Gradgrind,   15, 163

graphics,   22, 37, 59, 61, 75, 78, 80, 85, 121, 123 *see also,* computer graphics

Greek,   2

Griffin & George,   54

group dynamics,   135–137

group work,   52, 56, 75, 78, 88, 89, 90, 102, 115, 116, 124, 136, 137

Hadow Report, The,   xvi, 38–39, 177

handwriting,   44, 139

hardware,   16, 33, 60, 62, 68–69, 126, 166, 178

headteacher,   27

Henry VIII,   49

Her Majesty's Inspectorate (HMI),   21, 40, 41, 124, 141, 143

Herriott Watt University,   132, 178

Hertfordshire,   84, 143, 174

Higher Education, 15, 19, 168
histograms, 77, 78, 79
Historical Derivation, 143
history, 7, 12, 41, 47, 68, 73, 125, 131,
    133, 134, 136, 137, 138, 140
History project, 13-16, 143
History, Geography and Social Studies
    project, 67
Home Economics, 11, 165
Humanities, xvii, 19, 125-144, 163, 166
hypotheses, 11, 64-83, 94, 129, 133, 146,
    149, 153, 154, 161, 164, 165, 166

ideology, 7
Industrial Relation, 3
industry, 8
'inert ideas', 9
Infant Schools, xvii, 4, 21, 26, 29, 37-38,
    41, 108, 116, 117-122, 124
INFILE, 83, 178
information processing, 6, 22, 45, 46, 47,
    54, 61, 130, 131 see also, data processing
Information Studies, 23
Information Technology, 20, 21-23, 114,
    125, 139, 141-142
Initial Teaching Using Micros as an Aid
    (ITMA), 143, 178
Inner London Education Authority, 37,
    66, 83, 143, 173, 178
in - service education, 31, 60, 62, 87,
    114, 143
Institute of Education (University of
    London), 137, 174
Institute of European Education Graded
    Test Scheme, 143-144
integrated studies, 26, 131
intellectual development, xviii, 9, 12-13,
    18 see also, concept development
interests, 39, 40
Isle of Wight, 108

Julius Caesar, 108, 111
Junior Schools, 21, 24, 26, 29, 36-63, 64,
    83, 54, 106, 107-116, 117, 121-124

Lancaster, Joseph, 37
language, 40, 41, 53, 68, 90, 115, 116,
    121, 124, 131, 136, 143, 152, 153, 164
Latin, 2
learning process, 30
Leicester Education Authority, 83
liberal education, 1, 163

libraries, 26, 141, 142
literacy, 22
literary studies, 139
literature, 131
local advisory services, 21
local education authorities (LEAs), 59-60,
    62, 63, 143
logical thinking, 13
LOGO, xvii, xviii, 13, 17, 55, 63,
    84-106, 117, 120, 121-122, 124, 149,
    157, 165, 167-168, 178
LOGO challenge, 121-122, 178

Machine Stops, The, 6, 18
mainframe computers, 22, 25, 28, 138
manipulators skills, xiv
mapping, 44, 47, 50
Massachusetts Institute of Technology
    (MIT), 55, 87
mathematics, xvii, 11, 12, 24, 25-26, 28,
    41, 66, 68, 84-85, 89-106, 107-124,
    125, 130, 165, 166 see also, number
M'Chokumchild, 163
Microcomputers and Mathematics in
    Schools, 41-42, 124
Microcomputers in Education
    project, xvi, 60, 107, 114, 167, 174,
    178
Microelectronics Education
    Programme, 125, 126, 140, 143, 172
micro LEEP, 68, 69, 74, 83, 138, 178
Micro Primer pack, 114
MICROQUERY, 138, 178
micro SCAN, 83, 178
microtechnology, 3, 8, 9
Micro Users in Secondary Education
    (MUSE), 60
Middle Schools, 49, 83, 108
Milton Bradley Ltd, 151, 178
mixed ability classes, 89-90
modelling, 44, 47, 50
monitors, 37, 87, 94, 111, 112
moral education, 7, 9, 18
moral implications of
    microtechnology, 18-19, 67
motivation, 5, 6, 9-10, 25, 61, 86, 90,
    112, 138, 148, 157
multiplication, 112
music, 41, 59

National Association for the Teaching of
    English (NATE), 143

natural history, 47
Netherhall School, 143
New York, 122
1984, 18
Nineteenth Century Society, 72
Nuffield Foundation, 24
number, 37, 152, 153 *see also*,
  mathematics
numeracy, 22
Nursery Schools, 41

observation, 40
Observer, The, 107, 176
Open University, 142
Oracle, 142

pantograph, 47
physics, 4, 165
Piaget, xiv
plan, 39
Plato, 7
Plowden Report, The, xvi, 39, 177
political implications of
  microtechnology, 19
Practical Curriculum, The, 41
precis writing, 13, 50, 164
Presfax, 47, 50
Prestel, 6, 22
Primary Schools, xvi, xvii, 26–27,
  36–124, 127, 164
'Primary Survey', The, 40, 41, 177
principles, educational, 13–14
printers, 46, 68, 139, 179
problem-solving, 11, 22, 61, 89, 90, 93,
  98, 106, 111, 115, 150, 153
processors, xiv, xvi, 8–9, 10, 13, 52, 66,
  82, 115, 120, 145, 150, 164, 167
programmed learning, 36, 42, 61, 63,
  129, 147 *see also*, teaching machines
projects, 39, 41, 44, 52, 65, 66, 164 *see
  also*, topics
psychology, xviii, 5, 9, 12, 145, 146, 169
PUDDLE, 132, 178

QUERY, 83, 178
questioning, 9, 10, 11, 12, 15, 22, 69,
  106, 137, 138, 164

radio, 23
RAYBOX, 123, 178
reading, 17, 52, 59
Rectory Paddock School, 145

Registrar General, 67, 69
Research Machines Ltd, 68
resources, 141
RHINO, 122, 178
RML 3502, 68, 96
RML 4502, 96
role playing, 134, 135, 140
Romans, 108
rote learning, 37

School Curriculum, The, 40, 177
school journeys, 40
Schools Council, 24, 41, 67, 125, 143
school visits, 40
science, 24, 25, 28, 40, 41, 65, 66, 125,
  127, 131, 132, 143, 163, 164, 165, 166
scientific method, 65
Scylla and Charybdis, 63
Secondary Schools, xvii, xviii, 1, 4, 15,
  21, 24, 25, 26, 27, 29, 42, 55, 60, 67,
  84, 85, 107, 125–144, 168
sets, 38, 108
simulation, 61, 94, 129, 131–132, 133,
  134, 147, 150, 165
Sinclair User, 43
Skegness, 44
skills, 3, 8–9, 13, 17, 40, 44, 54, 55, 64,
  66, 68, 86, 111, 112, 114, 115, 117,
  139, 140, 145, 147, 148, 151, 158, 162
  see also, basic skills
slow learning children, 44, 59
social change, 3, 18
social class, 67, 69
social development, 9, 11, 18, 68
social dimension of learning, 5, 17–18
social implications of
  microtechnology, 18–19
social science, 73
Social Science Teacher, The, 64
social studies, 50, 52, 66–68, 82
society, 5, 18, 39, 169
Socrates, 164
software, 7, 33, 34, 36, 37, 47, 55, 59,
  60–61, 62, 63, 68–69, 96, 107, 112,
  125, 126, 127, 128, 129, 130, 130–135,
  136, 137, 138, 140, 142, 143, 144, 161,
  168, 177–179
solitary learning, 5–6, 7, 17–21
sound, 61
spatial concepts, xvii
Special Education, xviii, 4, 12, 145–161,
  169, 173

spelling, 60
Statistics Package for Social Sciences
    (SPSS), 138

TAKE HALF, 112, 178
teacher education, xvi, 31, 59, 62, 167 *see
    also*, in-service education
teaching machines, xiv, xviii, 5–7, 16, 17,
    54, 55, 114, 147, 169 *see also,*
    programmed learning
teleshopping, 22
teletext services, 21–22
television, 7, 10, 21, 23
    cable, 21
    educational, xiv, 5
    satellite, 21–22
Tertiary education, 127, 136, 138
textbooks, 7, 46
Times Educational Supplement, The, 39,
    59, 62
topics, 38, 41, 43, 44, 164 *see also,*
    projects
TRAY, 136
Turtles, xvii, xviii, 13, 53, 63, 86–106,
    117, 121, 149, 150, 151, 152, 154,
    156–157, 158, 159, 160, 161, 167, 168

understanding, 6, 9, 11, 12–13, 15–16,
    85, 102, 139, 141, 146, 147, 156, 164,
    165
user guides, 30, 32–33
utility, 1, 3, 163, 170

values, 7, 61
video games, xiv, 6, 134 *see also,*
    computer games
visual communications, 22
visual display unit (VDU), 10
vocational courses, 163, 170

'Weather', 53–54
WELCOME, 32
WINDS, 134, 178
woodwork, 17
word processing, 61, 139–140
Work, 66, 173
work cards/work sheets, 6–7, 7, 112, 129,
    142
WORKER, 132, 178
Worthing, 24
writing, 17, 40, 47, 50, 82

Zeaker, 55–57
ZX81, 88

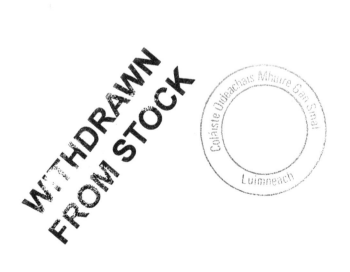